BILL PICKETT,
Bulldogger

BILL PICKETT, Bulldogger

The Biography of a Black Cowboy

By Colonel BAILEY C. HANES

With a foreword by
Bill Burchardt

UNIVERSITY OF OKLAHOMA PRESS : NORMAN AND LONDON

By Colonel Bailey C. Hanes

The Complete Bulldog (Richmond, Virginia, 1956)
The New Complete Bulldog (New York, 1966)
Bill Doolin, Outlaw O.T. (Norman, 1968)
The New Complete Bulldog, Third Edition (New York, 1973)
Bill Pickett, Bulldogger: The Biography of a Black Cowboy (Norman, 1977)

Library of Congress Cataloging-in-Publication Data

Hanes, Bailey C
   Bill Pickett, bulldogger.

   Bibliography: p. 187.
   Includes index.
   1. Pickett, Bill, 1860 (ca.)-1932. 2. Cowboys—
Biography. 3. Rodeos—United States. I. Title.
GV1833.6.P5H38   791.8[B]   76–54937
ISBN 0–8061–2203–X

TO KEVIN SCOTT HANES

My number one grandson

FOREWORD

By Bill Burchardt

Bill Pickett was the sum of many parts. That strangely intangible yet torrential force we call race was potent among them. Yet more potent was the admixture of inheritance and environment which forged him into a man larger than life, with attributes reminiscent of a mythological culture hero.

My article "A Rider of the 101" in the Autumn 1967 issue of *Oklahoma Today* magazine begins:

The steer lunged into the arena. The rider poised behind the barrier let the steer get a long running start then his horse plunged full speed after it.

Coming up on the steer's off side the rider leaped from the saddle. He turned a complete somersault along the length of the steer's back, flying out and down over the curved horns to fasten his teeth in the side of the steer's mouth.

With sheer strength he dragged the running behemoth's head to the tanbark, thrust its horn in the ground, and forward momentum threw the steer hocks over horns in a somersault of its own.

Whereupon the steer was altogether happy to lie quietly and rest awhile, with the bulldogger's teeth still biting its lip, his arms raised aloft to show that he had not used his hands at all, and the crowd in the grandstand which had fallen utterly silent, let loose a roar of applause and amazement. Bill Pickett had again performed his bulldogging act with the 101 Ranch Wild West Show.

Granted that Pickett did not perform his bulldogging act this way every time, but he performed it this way many, many times. This account was written from the contemporary eyewitness description of a *Tulsa World* newspaper reporter. The article is in the October 11, 1931, issue of the *World*, a conservative and dependable newspaper that maintains a high standard of careful observation and accuracy for its reporters.

Colonel Bailey C. Hanes and I have spent many enjoyable hours discussing the incredible Bill Pickett. A favored episode of ours is the time that Bill, himself Negro and Indian, was caught in Mexico in the cursh of two other racial cultures, Anglo and Spanish. An account of the event, set in large type and prominently displayed, was published in one of Mexico City's major newspapers of that time, *El Diavio*, on December 24, 1908. It is fascinating.

The article states that thirty years earlier it had been advertised to the public that they would see a brutal struggle between a Comanche Indian and a brave bull in the Plaza de Toros of the Paseo; that yesterday the public filled the plaza to witness a strange combat between a Negro from Oklahoma and the bull Bonito, a spectacle organized by the Miller brothers, owners of the 101 Ranch show that was performing in the Paseo de la Reforma; and that Governor Alfonso E. Bravo had intervened.

In place of the bull Bonito there appeared one from Tepeyahualco that did not have the respect and the bravery of the famous bull advertised. The newspaper account says that although the promoters had known in advance of the change to be made on orders of the governor, the public was not informed of this substitution. The audience protested loudly.

Bill Pickett did not enter the plaza alone, as it had been advertised that he would, but in the company of four riders who limited the action of the bull, cutting off its charges and keeping it in parentheses. Even then Pickett did not succeed in defeating the bull. The audience protested energetically. The lack of understanding, on both sides, could hardly have been more complete. The result was a tragic fiasco and an angry audience.

Anglo misunderstanding of the courtesies and traditions of the plaza were in that day equaled by Spanish misunderstanding of the customs of the rodeo arena, that hazers have to keep the animal to be bulldogged running in a straight line. How, also, do you like it when you pay admission to see something, then find that you're not going to see what the promoters promised you'd see?

Probably nothing is less understood among us than the bullfight. There is not even a Spanish word for it. In Mexico, in Spain, in South America, it is *la fiesta brava,* or a *corrida de toros,* a running of the bulls.

We lament the inhumanity of the bullfight, but if you were a bovine critter, consider which you would prefer: In the United States we throw a calf, brand him, maybe crop his ears, and perform on him an operation which makes him a steer. Then, while he is in the prime of life, we ship him to the slaughter-house. There, he is, by one means or another, killed and butchered. If you were a bull, would you prefer this fate, or would you prefer to take your chances in a bullfight?

What takes place in the Plaza de Toros is not a fight between a man and a bull; it is the encounter of a man and his own courage. What the matador must defeat is not the bull, but his own fear. A brave bull, truly a noble animal, is unlike his bovine kin. You will not really believe him until you see him. He is as agile as a goat. He exudes the sense of power of a locomotive running under a full head of steam (and he has the same sense of fear as a railroad locomotive). Behind him are more than a hundred generations of killers. Killing is his specialized knowledge, his desire, his skill, his purpose.

The people of Mexico vastly admire their brave bulls. They also admire the matadors who have the courage to stand still before them. They thought Bill Pickett and the 101 Ranch riders were insulting a brave bull in a degrading manner, that they were trying to ridicule the matador's courage. They demonstrated their anger in the same way U.S. audiences often do: they threw things. Pickett was hit by a deliberately thrown beer bottle. His horse was gored by the bull. Frustrated confusion became near riot, and the police had to be called in to settle things and protect the performers.

It seems incredible that the story of a man of Bill Pickett's stature could virtually sink from sight in a single generation, yet it has. We are emerging from an era which has buried the stories of many Americans of minority races: Negro, Indian, and others. The Bill Pickett story easily could have been lost completely. It has been badly warped in a good many magazine articles written by pseudohistorians and bigots intent on propaganda.

These are among the reasons why we especially value this book. Colonel Hanes is a dedicated and competent researcher. He has searched carefully and found original sources, rather than simply repeating old errors. He writes an exciting narrative. He has interviewed the living members of Bill Pickett's family, the old-time cowhands, the wild-west-show performers and early rodeo riders who knew Bill Pickett personally. We are thankful for historians like Colonel Hanes, and we commend to you his account.

PREFACE

This is a biography of Willie M. Pickett, professionally known as Bill, one of the world's most colorful and widely known Negro cowboys. Until now, a full account of him has not been published; rather, the writings about him have been concerned with some particular event in his life.

Few men have led a more exciting life than Pickett, who spent a large portion of his sixty years on the Miller Brothers' 101 Ranch at Marland, Oklahoma, and with the 101 Ranch Wild West Show. He was a legend in his own time: he invented and popularized a special type of bulldogging which led to the introduction of steer wrestling as one of the standard events in today's rodeo.

Information about this black cowboy, his life, and his accomplishments at a time when Oklahoma was young has been extremely difficult to find. Little was written then about Negroes, few family records were kept, and no one was especially interested in black history. So it was that I spent ten years gathering and evaluating the material from which this book was compiled, carefully sifting fact from fiction as I checked details against available documents or collected similar data from several sources. The result is as factual and accurate an account as can be written at this time.

To obtain it, I have relied on books; newspapers; periodicals; articles and other printed items; municipal, county, state, and family records; reminiscences of Pickett's contemporaries; and the verbal accounts of many people who knew him. I have intentionally omitted footnotes as unnecessary scholarly paraphernalia, but I have listed in the Bibliography all of the material I quote in the text.

I would take this opportunity to thank everyone who had a part in producing this book. I especially want to extend my appreciation to Fred Olds, well known southwestern artist and director of the Oklahoma Territorial Museum at Guthrie, Oklahoma, for his help; to Bill Burchardt, writer, historian and editor of *Oklahoma Today,* who wrote the Foreword; and to Milt Hinkle, who provided a great many facts and much color for the Pickett biography.

I extend my gratitude to Dr. J. Gordon Bryson, Walton Lewis, Fred Beeson, Sam Garrett, Jack D. Haley, Nannie Pickett Holmes, Ruth Pickett Ross, Alberta Pickett, Willie Wilson, Gareth Muchmore, Fred D. Pfening, Jr., the late Rev. W. Angie Smith, Johnny Mullins, Floyd Randolph, Sonny Schultz, and many other individuals who contributed material and encouragement to make this work possible.

COLONEL BAILEY C. HANES

Guthrie, Oklahoma

CONTENTS

ILLUSTRATIONS

BILL PICKETT,
Bulldogger

PROLOGUE

Of the hundreds of people, including celebrities, who either visited or rode for the Miller Brothers' 101 Ranch, none was more widely known, more respected, or more colorful than Bill Pickett, who spent more than a quarter-century of his life there. As a matter of record, Bill was the first man to bulldog cattle bite-'em style. He originated and perfected this trick to the point that modern rodeo is indebted to him for steer wrestling as a contest event. However, if one wishes to reach back into the dim recesses of history, one will find that Bill was not, strictly speaking, the world's first bulldogger.

Bull exhibitions date back to the Sumerians, prototypes of the earliest known civilized people, who lived in Babylonia (modern Iraq) some seven thousand years ago.

Cretans of the Minoan Culture (2900–1100 B.C.) held exhibitions in which both women and men participated: they somersaulted over the back of a bull. This sport can be traced back to about 2500 B.C.,

3

or almost forty-five hundred years ago. It has been suggested by historians that the Cretans may have learned it from an older Egyptian civilization that flourished between 5500 and 2000 B.C.

A sport involving bulls and men was popular in Cappadocia (present-day Turkey or Anatolia) about 2400 B.C. It involved grappling in which the man grabbed the horns of the bull.

Bulldogging almost identical to that seen in today's rodeos was practiced more than twenty-five hundred years ago in Thessaly, probably a remnant of the Cretan exhibitions. The Thessalians were superb horsemen in the arena. With ease and skill, a rider would jump from his horse, seize the horns of a bull, twist the animal's head, and throw the bull to the ground, much as is done today.

In more recent times, bulldogging was practiced in Rome during the reign of Julius Caesar (100–44 B.C.). In fact, it became so popular that Augustus Caesar (63 B.C.-A.D. 14), grandnephew of Julius, built the Statilus Taurus, the first Roman amphitheater designed specifically for the sport. Cattle, the ancestors of today's fighting bulls, were imported from Spain especially for bulldogging.

Since the late 1700's in England, the word *bulldogging* has been associated with the baiting, working, or holding of cattle—and sometimes hogs—by bulldogs. It has the same meaning in this country, and there are a number of references to bulldogs in western literature. Many butchers used them to handle stock (when I was a child, a butcher who operated a small packinghouse near our home had one). Most of the bulldogs in the early West—and there were many—were not purebreds but outcrosses, although they were nearly always referred to as bulldogs. Some of them weighed as much as eighty or ninety pounds and could hold a bovine by its upper lip with ease. Gradually, the word *bulldogging* was interpreted to mean "subduing or outdoing a steer by twisting him down by the horns."

The word *cowboy* is of uncertain origin. During the Revolutionary War, it was applied to armed Tories who tinkled cowbells to lure farmer patriots with lost cows into the brush, where the Tories ambushed them. Later, the word referred to Texas bandits who stole cattle from Mexicans, sometimes murdering the herders. Only after the Civil War did *cowboy* come to signify anyone who tended cattle in the West.

About one cowboy in every six or seven was Mexican; a similar proportion was black (most of the blacks had been slaves on Texas ranches, where they had been taught to ride and rope). Others were Indian or had some Indian blood. It has been estimated that at one time there were some four thousand Negro cowboys in Texas.

Rodeo is the evolutionary result of a cowboy's pride in his everyday job of working cattle. Naturally, it involves riding and roping, two skills in which cowhands tried to outdo one another when a common task brought them together during roundups and cattle drives. Impromptu riding-roping affairs were staged, too, at ranches and line camps to stave off the effects of a lonely existence.

It is not known when the first rodeo was held, but

5

by 1870, rangeland competition was common throughout the Southwest. Irish novelist Mydne Reid attended one at Santa Fe, New Mexico Territory, in June 1846. In his account, which is probably the earliest written record of a rodeo, he used the words *round-up* and *cowhand*, a very early date for them.

One of the classics of intercamp cowboy competition was the bronc-busting contest held on July 4, 1869, at Deer Trail, Colorado Territory. The best horsemen in the territory entered. The rules of the contest stipulated that the horses were to be ridden with a slick saddle; that is, the saddle must be free from the roll usually tied across the horse, the stirrups must not be tied under the animal, and the rider must not wear spurs. The horses selected for the contest were outlaws—impossible to break—and this made it extremely dangerous.

One young cowpuncher by the name of Will Goff vowed he would "ride anything with hair on it." A gentle-looking bay horse was led out. Goff pulled off his coat, threw his suspenders aside, took a reef in his belt, and with one bound landed on the bay's back. Swish! His felt hat whistled through the air and caught the bronc across the side of the head. The pony pitched violently for fifty yards, making about three hundred revolutions to the minute. Then he started to run and the crowd howled. "Give me my spurs and I'll make him pitch," yelled Goff. He was given his spurs, and he cut the pony to bits. The exhibition was not satisfactory, however, because the rider had too easy a time.

Another cowboy, Drury Grogan, tackled a sorrel pony which carried the Camp Stool brand. As soon as the horse was saddled and Drury was on its back, it pitched, plunged, kicked, and seesawed, but it did not unseat the cowboy, who made a successful ride and was awarded with the applause and cheers of the crowd.

The next rider was an Englishman, Emilnie Gardenshire, from the Mill Iron Ranch. He drew Montana Blizzard, a bay horse from the Hashknife Ranch. Rawhide whip in hand, Gardenshire crawled aboard cautiously. Once he was firm in his seat, he began to larrup the bay unmercifully, and there followed a sight which tickled the spectators hugely. The Englishman rode with hands free and kept plying his whip constantly. There was a frightful mixup of cowboy and horse, but Gardenshire refused to be unseated. For fifteen minutes the bay bucked, pawed, and jumped from side to side. Then, amid cheers, the mighty Blizzard succumbed, and Gardenshire rode him around the circle at a gentle gallop. For this magnificent piece of horsemanship, the cowboy from the Mill Iron Ranch won a title, Champion Bronco Buster of the Plains, and a prize, a suit of clothes.

On July 4, 1883, the folks in Pecos, Texas, staged a celebration and asked area cowboys to bring a contest to town. They did. Longhorn steers were penned in the yard of the courthouse, and the cowhands roped them on the run down Pecos' main street. In Texas, however, rodeos have been held on both sides of the Río Grande at El Paso since the early 1880's.

Prescott Arizona, is credited with staging the first commercial rodeo. Called Frontier Days, it was held in 1888. Organizers charged admission and offered cash prizes to the winners. The Frontier Days celebration at Cheyenne, Wyoming, followed in 1897. Then came the Round-Up at Pendleton, Oregon, in 1910 and Canada's Calgary Stampede in 1912. These four rodeos have been held annually since they were first performed and are widely known throughout the world.

The wild west show helped to establish rodeo and whet the public's appetite for cowboy sports. It was the brainchild of William F. Cody, who, with the help of W. F. Carver, launched the Buffalo Bill and Dr. Carver's Wild West Show in 1883. Many wild west shows followed, the most noteworthy of which probably were Buffalo Bill's Wild West and Congress of Rough Riders of the World, Buffalo Bill's Wild West and Pawnee Bill's Far East Combined, the Tom Mix Circus and Wild West, Colonel Zack Mulhall's Wild West, Pawnee Bill's Historic Wild West, and, of course, the greatest and most spectacular of them all, the Miller Brothers' 101 Ranch Wild West Show (1907–1916 and 1925–1931). The Miller extravaganza was first called the Miller Brothers' 101 Ranch Wild West Show, later became the Miller Brothers' 101 Ranch Real Wild West Show, and finally was known as the Miller Brothers' 101 Real Wild West and Great Far East Show. It went broke in Washington, D.C., on August 5, 1931, and was never able to make a come-back.

Even in the heyday of the wild west shows, rodeo was gradually eating away at their popularity, and the ever increasing cost of operation spelled their doom. They had all but faded from the scene by the 1930's, and the few attempts to revive them in the

1940's were failures. Most of the shows' participants were working cowboys who competed in rodeos throughout the country, and they were some of the best because they practiced all the time.

With the demise of the wild west shows, rodeo took over in earnest. By 1975, well over 500 rodeos were being held annually in the United States, and professional cowboys were winning as much as $8,898 at a single rodeo, $38,118 annually in a single event, and $63,000 annually by entering more than one event (Bill Linderman, rodeo cowboy de luxe, won $443,013 during his career). In 1973, contestants in rodeos sanctioned by the Rodeo Cowboys Association won more than $4,000,000. Rodeo was one of the nation's leading spectator sports that year, drawing more than 16,000,000 viewers. It ranked with basketball, baseball, auto racing, football, and horse racing in total attendance and led boxing, hockey, wrestling, and soccer.

A rodeo is made up of seven standard events: steer wrestling (bulldogging), saddle bronc riding, bareback bronc riding, bull riding, calf roping, steer roping, and team roping. Saddle bronc riding, steer roping and calf roping are direct developments of ranch work and were the only original rodeo events. The others are the result of a need for other ways to compete and were invented in the arena. Among them, only bulldogging can be traced to the creativity of an individual, in this instance Bill Pickett. The other events came from the ingenuity of many men whose names have been lost in the dust of time.

Steer wrestling has no tie with everyday ranch duties

and was not used as a rodeo event until 1910. Before that time, steers were bulldogged at rodeos, cowboy contests, county fairs, and wild west shows, but usually only as an exhibition. However, evidence suggests that bulldogging may have been used as a contest as early as 1903. Whatever the case, Bill Pickett's daring display of skill in steer wrestling—downing the animal by biting its upper lip—at rodeos and performances of the 101 Ranch Wild West Show caught the eye and fancy of the public. Other cowboys saw its possibilities, and as more and more of them began to try it, dogging developed into a regular rodeo contest. Among the cowboys who copied Pickett's bite-'em style were Milt Hinkle, Lon Seeley, Ralph Whitlock, Wild Jim Lynch, Joe Pickett (a Negro cowboy, not related to Bill), Buffalo Vernon, Shorty Kelso, Frank "Scout" Maish, Mike Hastings, Jim Massey, and Fred Spain. All were working cowboys and wild west show performers, and most of them worked for the Miller brothers at one time or another. Fox Hastings, a red-head with muscles like a man's, was the first woman bulldogger. Smokey Hester and Claire Belcher were two other early-day girl doggers.

Available records list Lon Seeley as the first white man to bulldog a steer professionally Pickett style. He used Pickett's horse, Spradley, at the Jamestown (Virginia) Exposition in 1907, performing the feat for a full week while Pickett was recovering from a bull-dogging injury. Seeley's career did not last long. In October, 1908, while he was with the 101 Ranch Wild West Show in Gulfport, Mississippi, he killed and was killed by a deputy sheriff in a case of mistaken iden-

Bill Pickett bulldogging with his teeth.

tity. As they passed down a dark alley, both men drew their guns and fired simultaneously. Seeley is buried in Gulfport.

Milt Hinkle was the second white man to bulldog professionally Pickett style and was perhaps the first white man to dog a steer Pickett style on a ranch. He was told of Pickett's feat in the fall of 1904 and was encouraged by Booger Red Privett to try it. A short time later at the XIT Ranch at Bovina, Texas, Hinkle was successful in his first attempt to dog a steer bite-'em style. He bulldogged a steer from a small airplane near Plainview, Texas, in 1920, and in 1929 at Nuevo

Laredo, Mexico, he dogged another from a Ryan airplane (a sister ship to Colonel Charles A. Lindbergh's *Spirit of St. Louis*).

Among other things, Hinkle was a rodeo announcer and promoter, wild-west-show performer, cowhand, and rodeo contestant. He knew and worked with Bill Pickett off and on for more than a quarter of a century. His father, George, was a buffalo-hide buyer who during the winter tended bar at Hoover's Saloon (next door to the Long Branch) in Dodge City, Kansas. George served as sheriff of Ford County, Kansas, from 1880 to 1884 after moving there from Texas. Milt was born on October 15, 1881, in a dugout on the Bovina Division of the XIT. This Texas ranch, the largest in the world, embraced three million acres of land, covered ten counties, and belonged to the Farrell brothers of Chicago, Illinois (Milt says the X stood for *ten*, the I for *in*, the T for *Texas*—ten counties in Texas).

The name of Fred Spain was quite prominent in the early days of Oregon's Pendleton Round-Up. He and his brother John helped to promote the event and furnished part of the stock. The outstanding buckers Hot Foot and Going Some were both Spain horses. About 1911, Fred was bulldogging at Pendleton and using his teeth to hold the steer while he raised both hands for time. Pickett's bite-'em style was spreading.

On June 15, 1939, Associated Press carried a story, datelined Yakima, Washington, about Alex McCoy (Owl Child), a Yakima Indian, who, the story said, invented bulldogging while working as a cowboy for Ben Snipes, an early-day Yakima Valley cattleman.

This is quite possible, but the event probably occurred long after Bill Pickett dogged his first steer. It should be noted, however, that McCoy made no claim to the Pickett feat. Apparently, McCoy bulldogged at early rodeos in the Northwest, but rodeo was not introduced there until the early twentieth century and Pickett dogged his first steer in the 1880's.

Today, steer wrestling is one of the most popular rodeo events, and bulldoggers have earned as much as $30,715 in a single year—a far cry from Bill Pickett's $8 to $12 per week dogging with the 101 Ranch Wild West Show. Times are faster, too, for a number of reasons; shorter barriers and smaller steers are two of them. As of 1974, the best official time was George Mill's 2.1 seconds, with Oral Harris Zumwalt's 2.2 seconds a close second. Pickett's best official time as a contestant was 8 seconds flat—only a second off the world record for the year. Both were recorded at the Cattleman's Carnival, a rodeo held at Garden City, Kansas, on September 7, 8, and 9, 1916. In 1937 at Salt Lake City, Utah, Hugh Bennett and Dave Campbell dogged their steers in 3.2 seconds—close to the top of the list for fast time.

Bill Pickett may have been slow, but he did more for rodeo bulldogging than any other man. In every respect, he was a working cowboy (the only Negro in the five-hundred-member Cherokee Strip Cowpunchers Association) and a performer (universally recognized by the fraternity as the progenitor of the only standard rodeo event that can be traced to a single individual). He has been cited as the inventor of rodeo bulldogging, and he was the first cowboy to bulldog more than five thousand head of cattle in the arena and on the range. Were it not for Pickett, the development of steer wrestling in rodeo might have come much later.

⌇ I ⌇

A STAR IS BORN

On October 9, 1854, an emigrant party of South Carolinians headed west for Texas. The caravan was made up of one hundred hardy souls: forty-eight whites and fifty-two Negro slaves. The white families were represented by John Russell, the Bartons, the Pools, and the Goodlets. The Bartons are the only kinship group due further mention in this biography, that because of their Negro slaves.

The Barton segment was headed by Welborn Barton, a country doctor, and his brother, Colonel Alexander Barton; it is not known how or where Alexander received his military-sounding title. A good percentage of the fifty-two slaves in the expedition belonged to this wealthy family. Some of them answered, by Southern custom, to the surnames of their owners, but at least two of the black families, headed by brothers, were known as Pickett. Their name may have been derived from the name of some former master and their new owners, the Bartons, allowed them to retain it.

Black Bartons and Picketts were related by marriage. Pickett family tradition holds that the ancestral namesakes were of mixed Negro, Caucasian, and Cherokee Indian blood, a not uncommon blend in the Upper South. Contemporary descendants of the two Pickett brothers do not know the given names of any forebears. The Texas Census Report for 1880 states that Thomas Jefferson Pickett was born in Louisiana and was twenty-six years old in 1880, which means that one of the Pickett women was pregnant at the time the wagons headed west and that he was born at some unknown place in 1854 as the caravan passed through Louisiana.

The weather was excellent, and after two weeks of travel the emigrants stopped to visit relatives, catch up on washing, and repair wagons. After a brief layover, the long journey was resumed. Nearly all of the wagons were new. They were covered with carriage cloth and had roll-up curtains equipped with buttons so that no rain could enter. The travelers followed the lower route, which traversed all the large rivers. They crossed the Mississippi on a steamboat near Natchez at a point where the river was one and one-fourth miles wide. The next crossing was on the Red River at Alexandria, Louisiana, where a second steamboat served as ferry. Then on to the Sabine River and over into Texas and its dreary-looking acres with nothing in sight but live oaks covered with plumes of Spanish moss.

The South Carolinians circled around the town of Sabine but passed through Palestine, Nacogdoches, Crockett, and several other small towns before they

arrived in Washington-on-the-Brazos, Texas' first capital city. The next stop was at Old Independence in
Washington County. A part of Christmas week was
spent in the Gay Hill neighborhood with relatives
of the Bartons, Russells, and Goodlets. From there
the newcomers pushed on to Williamson County,
where they met their old Carolina friends the Brysons.
Here they camped for the remainder of the winter.
In the spring, they bought land in the western quarter
of the county, and settlement began in earnest. The
subsection lay in the foothills of the great Edwards
Plateau, which embraces much of Central Texas; it
was a wide stretch of small peaks and brushy hillocks,
with neither contour nor soil structure suiting it for
cotton, a product that grows best on level lands. Yet
its rocky natural pastures afforded good grass for livestock raising, once brush and cactus were removed.
Barring one of Texas' savage droughts, there was
plenty of water in creeks, springs, and the convenient
San Gabriel River.

There were probably too many rattlesnakes and
horse thieves, and occasionally Comanche Indians still
came raiding from the faraway Staked Plains of West
Texas, but their depredations were decreasing. Settlers roundabout were English-speaking Anglo-Saxon
and Scotch-Irish Southerners of familiar creeds, but
many of them were staunchly opposed to the Seces-
sionist tendencies of the planter aristocracy.

Wild horses and cattle, both susceptible to domesti-
cation, abounded in the groves and thickets. Feed
crops, such as corn and oats, could be grown with
fair success. Like the rest of Williamson County, this

semi-mountainous strip lay within the immediate orbit of Austin, the growing state capital and seat of adjoining Travis County.

On a large tract about three miles from the Travis County line, the Bartons settled with their slaves of both surnames, including the infant Tom Pickett. Here they helped form a community, later known as Jenks-Branch, which is today composed mostly of the descendants of former slaves. Records of the Texas General Land Office show that the Barton place paralleled the south bank of the San Gabriel River, a pretty stream coursing through banks of white limestone. The family's supply source and post office address was a Williamson County village, Liberty Hill, that is still in existence. Dr. Barton undoubtedly undertook some medical practice, since the needs of the people made it hard for a frontier physician to retire. According to oral accounts, he and his brother were also prospering farmers and stockmen.

The adult slaves had been used to work livestock in South Carolina. Their Texas-born children naturally learned such skills as horse breaking and cattle branding. Interviews with living family members indicate that even then there was a strong and constant tradition of what would come to be called cowboying. Spurs and lariats seemed to have been as familiar to them as rakes and hoes to their ancestors.

When the Civil War erupted in 1861, Tom Pickett was too young to understand why Texas, with its Southern tradition, withdrew from the Union. Perhaps he had greater comprehension when the proud Confederacy crumbled in 1865 and its slaves were at last truly emancipated. Most of the freed Barton and Pickett slaves remained in the hill country in the vicinity of Jenks-Branch, which straddled the border between Travis and Williamson counties. The community probably was named for two early landowners, John W. Jenks and John W. Branch. An 1890 Travis County map shows a number of small plots occupied by Picketts and Bartons.

In 1879, Jerry Poinsett Barton and Anderson Pickett, cousins (and cousins of Bill Pickett), participated in a cattle drive. Their employer was Thomas S. Snyder. He and his brothers, Dudley Hiram and John W., were prominent early-day Texas cattlemen. These two black Texans who worked for them deserve honorable mention in the long list of Negro cowboys, estimated to number five thousand by western author and historian William B. Secrest. The Snyders, who came from Mississippi, were among the pioneer families of Williamson County. Thomas married Lenora A. Bryson in 1867.

Tom bought 2,525 cattle from John Green of Victoria County for $10,000. At Liberty Hill on March 10, 1879, he put together an outfit that was to go to Green's ranch, round up the cattle, and trail them north to Dodge City, Kansas, over the Chisholm Trail (five hundred miles from Fort Worth to Dodge City). The herd passed near Austin, Fort Worth, and Denton before crossing the Red River into Indian Territory and pressing north to Rock Creek Crossing on the Washita River, through Silver City on the South Canadian, then through Caddo Springs, the Dover Stage Stand, Buffalo Springs, and on to Dodge City.

The outfit consisted of Snyder, trail boss George Arnett, eight cowboys, a cook, and a team and a wagon. Anderson Pickett, Jerry Barton, Sam Allen, Joe Felder, Andy Marcus, John Ledbetter, John Fletcher, and Will Bower were the cowboys. They hired a guide en route, one Jim Andrews, and bought saddle horses as they traveled south to Victoria. Pickett served as Snyder's aide, rode herd in his turn, and otherwise took care of Snyder's personal needs. At Hutto, Snyder turned the trail herd over to Arnett and returned to Liberty Hill. Pickett also left and signed up with an outfit trailing horses to Wyoming. Barton completed the drive. In the early 1900's, Barton married his childhood sweetheart, Patsy Miller, daughter of the well known and respected Aunt Easter Miller.

Thomas Jefferson Pickett seems to have felt no longings for distant places and a rugged life. In 1870 in Travis County, he married Mary Virginia Elizabeth Gilbert. Family records state Willie M. Pickett was born at Jenks-Branch community, about thirty miles northwest of Austin in Travis County, on December 5, 1870. The Travis County Census Report of June 2, 1880, correctly lists his father's birthplace as Louisiana and lists the son's age as eight, which would indicate that Willie was born in 1871 (birth dates are not shown in this document). On the basis of available information, then, it can be assumed that Willie was born in 1871, and that is the date of birth I have accepted. As he grew to manhood, he was known to his friends as Bill and during his later life, he was known as Uncle Bill.

Information about Bill Pickett's early life and his family is scant, but all I have been able to piece together follows. Bill was one of thirteen children born to Tom and Mary (she was also called Janie) Pickett. Descendants say Mary, who was small and very dark, was of Negro, Mexican, Caucasian, and Indian extraction. Tom and Mary named their children Charles H., Willie M., Henrietta E., Benny W., Jessie J., Mary J., Channie S., Clara, Lucile, Leala Maud, Alice M., Ethel C., and Berry F. All thirteen were born in Travis or Williamson counties between 1870 and 1890. Dates of birth for the children born after Mary J. are unreliable, but family and census records verify the number of children, their names, and the dates between which they were born.

Sometime in the early 1870's, Tom Pickett moved into or near Austin (the date of the move also has gone unrecorded), where he rented a small tract and raised vegetables to sell in the capital city. Occasional odd jobs brought in supplemental income, but the total earnings from those extra tasks could not have been very large during an era when standard wages for Negros were less than fifty cents a day.

From the time he began walking, Bill was the standout of the growing but impoverished family. He was short, stout, very active, and extremely curious. He was outgoing, had a flowing sense of humor, and was always alert for a chance to earn a nickel or a dime from some chore or errand.

At some time in his childhood, he entered school for what proved to be a very limited education: he finished the fifth grade. The name of the school is not known, but it probably was a rural one, since the names of the Pickett children do not appear on the rolls of Austin's first Negro public school. Wheatville

School was located north of College Hill and west of San Gabriel, which suggests that the Picketts must have lived in a rural section outside the city's boundaries. Bill's school probably was typical of those built for black pupils: a wooden, one-room, one-teacher affair, cheaply constructed and burdened with a poor curriculum. It functioned only four or five months each year because Negro and poor white children alike were needed to chop cotton in mid-spring and pick it in the fall. Moreover, the idea of anything beyond a meager education for black children was an unpopular one in the former Confederacy.

There was another form of learning in Texas, one not taught from books and blackboards. It could be acquired handily by any youngster with the necessary knack. Its only literacy requirement was being able to read horse and cattle brands correctly. Bill Pickett began acquiring this system of knowledge, known as cowboying, from both his family heritage and the hectic, bustling, workaday atmosphere of Austin and the surrounding ranches.

In a classic sense Austin had become almost typically another western cow town. The transition from an overgrown rural community began when Texas started wresting itself from the shambles of Reconstruction by marching its wild Longhorns to the railroads and beef markets of the Middle West. Columns of bawling, cowboy-directed cattle were familiar sights on Congress Avenue, the capital's broad main street. Austin matrons were angered often by invasions of stray steers that devoured their flowers and shrubs. Farmers cursed because hitching posts, erected for their wagon teams, were monopolized by cow ponies. Cattle buyers and sellers thronged the avenue to arrange lucrative trades usually sealed by word and handshake. Successful cowmen, such as Colonel Jesse Lincoln Driskill and Major George W. Littlefield, were numbered among the town's leading and wealthiest citizens.

Major Littlefield, who was also a banker, headed the Littlefield Cattle Company, which owned and operated a large ranch near Austin under the LFD brand. Driskill, another widely known Texan who ranched in the Austin area, was among the first cattlemen to point 'em north to Dodge City. He built the Driskill Hotel, an Austin landmark.

Hardware and general-merchandise stores profited from the sale of saddles, guns, spurs, lariats, rope, castrating knives, and other accessories of the booming cow business. The Lone Star State's great main hoofway, the Texas Trail, crossed Austin's eastern outskirts at the spot now occupied by a municipal airport. From there, it wound around the northwest edge of the Austin city limits before plunging north to join the equally historic Chisholm Trail at Red River Crossing on the boundary of Indian Territory.

Like many another lad, Willie M. Pickett was fascinated by cowboys. Unlike most small fry, however, his interest extended beyond popping a toy gun and wearing mail-order cowboy suits. His curiosity about cowboys made him keenly observant of their work habits: how they broke and shod mustangs for saddle mounts, how they swung lariats in precise patterns and with exact timing to encircle an animal's neck, how they herded and branded wild Longhorns rounded up from vast open ranges, creatures possessing slashing defense equipment and of no mind to become steaks on dinner tables.

The cattle age moved forward with the rumbling echoes of more and more hoofs making the long trek overland; it created its own legends, circulated by working cowboys and plain old windjammers. Down in Texas, a little black boy continued to identify with the men who moved the cattle and repeated the legends. He listened in worshipful admiration to the tales spun by his cousins Anderson Pickett and Jerry Barton, for they had experienced the stuff of which the legends were made. They had swallowed the choking dust on long jaunts to Kansas. They had known the sogging chill of sudden rains, the pounding fury of hail, the rumbling crash of thunderstorms. Across the Red River, they had herded dripping-wet steers into wide preserves of grass owned by the Indian nations. Their ears had been bombarded by the terrifying thunder of stampedes and the sharp crack of gunfire exchanged with rustlers and Indians who followed trail herds to steal cattle. They had ridden down the streets of faraway towns to deliver stock to waiting trains of cattle cars headed east. They had lived to tell it all. To recount their experiences at family gatherings in Jenks-Branch. Or to render scraps of adventure when they came visiting Cousin Tom Pickett's household on the outskirts of Austin.

Willie M. Pickett dreamed of doing all those heroic things he attributed to his relatives. The Pickett-Barton connection now had three cowboys: two adults decked in polished boots and spurs, and a barefoot boy filled with visions of grandeur.

Young Bill Pickett's interest in cattle operations often caused him to loiter on the way to school. Finally, he could read accurately any brand on steer or cow. He learned how to toss a lariat and how to stay atop a recently broken mustang that was still resenting sting of spur and clamp of bit. On a day in 1881 that was to have unforeseen potential, he happened to notice a bulldog holding a cow motionless by her upper lip. The dog's fangs apparently were quite painful to the sensitive membranes because their tenacious grip made the captive animal submissive. Yet the whole procedure was probably less cruel to the animal than the abrupt choking squeeze of a lariat.

Many early-day Texas ranchers kept cow dogs to help work wild cattle out of thickets, where they hid from cowboys. Such dogs were usually half or more English bulldog; the rest might be a cross with any other breed or perhaps just plain dog. They usually weighed fifty to sixty pounds, and many were predominantly white or brindle. Their ancestors were used in England for fighting and bullbaiting. Some were even used to bait lions and bears.

Wise old cattle would stand perfectly still and hide out in the thick brush. If brushers showed fight or would not be driven out of their hiding places, the ranchers would issue a command to their trained bulldogs to go get 'em. That command was all that was needed for the dogs to catch and hold the largest, wildest fighting bull, cow, steer calf, or any other animal they were ordered to catch.

One was known as the heel dog; it ran in and nipped at the heels of the animal, drawing attention away from a second dog, known as the catch dog. When the animal started to fight off the heel dog, the catch dog made its move and secured a death hold on the animal's upper lip. The animal would be held in this fashion until the cowhands could get a rope on it, after which it was tied up or dragged from the thicket by a cow pony. Sometimes the animal was necked to a gentle ox or steer trained for this purpose. It was left tied thus until it became tame enough to turn out with the rest of the cattle and would stay put.

In the early days in Texas, this process was called bulldogging. Gone forever are the bulldogs of that day, the old mossback cattle, and that breed of rough-and-ready cowmen who worked the vast open range. As Bill Pickett watched on that eventful day in 1881, the wearisome bulldog finally released the scared cow and trotted off. During the days that followed, the boy kept reflecting on the incident. If a dog of much less weight could subdue a grown cow with a nose hold, why couldn't a man do the same? Or, in proportion to size, why couldn't a calf be held by a boy?

A few days later, Bill walked up to a calf and grabbed it by the ears with his hands. The animal squirmed and bawled, trying to free itself. Bill then fastened his teeth on the calf's upper lip, turned loose of its ears, and, with a flip of his body, threw it to the ground.

The first opportunity Bill had to put his newly acquired skill to a practical use came on the way to school one day. He had to pass a group of Littlefield

Cattle Company cowboys branding calves, and they were having quite a time holding some of the larger ones. Bill watched for a while, then volunteered the information that he could hold the calves with his teeth. This statement was taken lightly by the cowboys, and they got a good laugh out of it. However, to promote some sport, one of the cowboys suggested that they let the kid try to hold one of the calves while it was being branded; they had a pretty good idea what would happen. One of them roped and threw a calf, one of the largest still unbranded, and invited Bill to hold the animal while they proceeded with the branding. Bill carefully got his bulldog hold and waved to the cowboys to turn the calf loose, which they were eager to do in order that the show might start. Much to their surprise, the calf scarcely made a sound or moved a muscle as the hot branding iron was applied to its tender hide. Given the signal to turn loose, Bill let go and the animal scrambled to its feet and ran off to rejoin the other calves. The cowboys were amazed and soon spread the word around Austin that the Pickett kid could bulldog a calf while it was being branded. Thus began a legend that was to grow into one of the most colorful realities of the sports world in the twentieth century.

Bill Pickett and two of his brothers in the 1890's. Bill is seated.

⚞ II ⚟

THE YEARS IN TAYLOR

After completing the fifth grade and graduating from many boyhood chores, Bill Pickett began to work on ranches in the vicinity of Austin. He learned to ride and rope and seemed to be a natural when it came to working livestock. When he was fifteen or sixteen, he began riding broncs on Sunday afternoons for the amusement of onlookers. It was his custom to pass his battered hat among the spectators, and in this way he kept spending money in his pocket.

Bill first practiced bulldogging cows and steers that were running wild in the mesquite brush. The brush was so thick that it was almost impossible to build a loop and lasso with any degree of efficiency, so he did the next-best thing: ride alongside a running steer, lean over, and jump from the saddle, catch the steer by its long horns, twist its head and throw the animal to the ground. He soon discovered that he could use his old bite-'em trick, both to down a steer and to hold it as long as he wished.

It was during his sixteenth year that Bill was watching a group of Texas cowboys attempt to round up a small herd of wild steers near Austin. They were having little success; most of the steers eluded the ropes and returned to the brush. A number of well-known old-time cowhands were in the crew: Frate Barker, Morgan Lewis, Jim Lucas, Riley Smith, Emsey Baker, and Bill Brown. Pickett made the observation that "I can catch and hold them with my teeth" when he saw how many of the steers got away and disappeared into the mesquite. "Let him try it" was Bill Brown's answer to the outlandish offer. In short order, Pickett caught and threw three steers in succession.

Shortly after dogging the three steers for Brown, Pickett was asked to go to Nashville, Tennessee, to the Confederate Soldiers Reunion to ride and bulldog with a wild west show that was being put together for entertainment. Bill agreed to go. When he bulldogged a steer with his teeth, the men in gray were amazed because they considered such a feat impossible.

In the late 1880's, Thomas Jefferson Pickett moved a second time: to Taylor, Williamson County, Texas. On October 18, 1888, he bought Lots 1 and 2, Block 77, from John S. Borues *et al.* for one hundred twenty-seven dollars. The property, located at 811 East Second Street, remained the family home for many years.

Taylor was and is in the center of one of Texas' richest agricultural sections. The fertile black soil produced above-average crops of cotton and corn, and excellent pastures fed fine hogs, sheep, and cattle. The town had a population of twenty-five hundred, its own water system, free public schools, and was served by three railroads, all of which had extensive shops there. The International & Great Northern ran east and west; The Missouri Pacific (later the Missouri, Kansas & Texas) ended at Taylor; the Taylor, Bastrap & Houston had been completed only from Taylor to Bastrap when the Picketts moved there.

Taylor boasted a national bank, several good hotels, and sixteen brick business buildings in addition to many frame structures. There were fourteen dry-goods and grocery stores, three drugstores, two furniture stores, five saloons, two hardware stores, a bookstore, two boot-and-shoe houses, two saddle-and-harness shops, two butcher shops, four blacksmith shops, one Chinese laundry, two lumberyards, two corn-and-cotton mills and gins, two barbershops, two bakeries, five church buildings, an opera house, an Odd Fellows hall, and a Masonic hall. The restaurant-saloon-bakery, located where the Owl Cafe later operated for years, was owned by Fritz Lange. The largest saloon was the Golden Rule, which had a back room for gambling; Bud Saul's Saloon was its chief competitor. Negroes operated the two barbershops. Taylor's main street was so muddy when it rained that wagons bogged down. There were hitching posts along Main Street in front of each store, and the sidewalks—where there were sidewalks—were made of boards. This was the Taylor that greeted the Picketts in 1888 upon their arrival from Austin.

During the next several years, Bill Pickett worked for a number of ranches in the Taylor, Georgetown, and Round Rock areas of Williamson County and the Rockdale area of Milam County. He first worked on the J. M. Kuykendall ranch, then with Emsey Baker on the Governor E. Sparks ranch fourteen miles southeast of Taylor on Brushey Creek. He also worked at the Stells O. Sorrow ranch, the Hickest ranch, Lee Moore's ranch near Rockdale, the Garrett E. King ranch, Turkey Creek Ranch five miles northeast of Taylor, and the Buck Wills ranch. When he worked for King, he loved to jump from the cross brace of the corral gate onto the back of the ranch mules and ride them to a standstill or until he was thrown off. Bill could hold and bridle any horse or mule if he could get close enough to catch its ear. If the beast was too wild, he simply grabbed the ear between his teeth and held on. This method has been used by cowboys as long as there have been cowboys and wild horses.

In 1889, Buck Wills, owner of the Buck Wills Saloon in Taylor, hired Bill to feed and work cattle on his Williamson County ranch. The pay was five dollars per week, and some weeks stretched to eighty-four working hours. There were no fringe benefits, coffee breaks, or paid vacations. On January 10, during the especially severe winter of 1892-93, Bill froze both of his feet in his boots as he was working cattle; fortunately, he did not lose any toes. During the same winter, he caught three wolves and two foxes that were stealing calves and chickens. An expert in both, he hunted and fished the year round to help keep food on the table for the large Pickett family.

While he lived in Texas, Bill had several good cow horses, among them Hope, Sparkie, Blue Bird, Chico, and Cropper, his favorite. Cropper was so named because he had one cropped ear. It was common practice in the range country to earmark stock, and sometimes the method was used on stock that was also branded.

At Taylor in the late 1880's, Bill met Maggie Turner of Palestine, Anderson County. Maggie was the daughter of Sherman Turner, a white southern plantation owner, and her mother was Turner's former Negro slave. Bill and Maggie began seeing each other, and after a beautiful romance, they were married in Taylor by a Baptist minister, A. S. Scott, on December 2, 1890. (Their marriage license erroneously lists Maggie's maiden name as Williams. That was the name of her stepfather.) Bill and Maggie made their home in Taylor and reared their family there. They had nine children: Sherman, Nannie, Bessie, Leona, Boss, Willie, Kleora Virginia, Almarie, and Alberdia. Sherman and Boss failed to survive their first birthdays, but all of the girls lived to adulthood.

Bill was for many years a deacon in the Taylor Baptist Church. At one time, for lack of a building, Sunday school and church services were held in an upstairs room of the Pickett home. Meanwhile, Bill continued to work for Buck Wills and to hunt and fish. He very often hunted without a dog and mostly at night, carrying only a light, rope, and a knife. As his first three daughters grew old enough, he sometimes took them along. He caught coons, possums, and fish and, to help supplement his income, cooked them for the free lunch served at the Buck Wills Saloon. In the fall, he picked cotton; on a good day, he could pick more than 500 pounds.

In the late 1890's, Bill got something in his eyes and was blind for 11 months. His third daughter,

Leona, led him around. After he recovered, he was never bothered with his eyes again.

The directors of the Williamson County Livestock Association met in 1887, organized, and made plans for a fair at Taylor in the spring of 1888. The fairgrounds site was some distance south of Taylor and covered a large level area on top of a hill. It was an ideal place for rodeos. There were no fences around it because there were very few fences in those days. Stake-and-rider rail fence was about all folks had.

The first Taylor fair was held on schedule in 1888 at the new fairgrounds, and one of the attractions was a rodeo. Dave Young, a boy of twelve at the time, states:

The Baker Boys were the ropers and bronc riders. . . . They gave us boys calves to rope but not tie. When we caught a calf some of the men would come, turn it loose for us. It was at this Fair that Tom and Will Pickett made their first exhibition of bulldogging a steer. After the steer had been roped and tied down, then when they turned it loose either Tom or Will Pickett would straddle the steer. When he would fight and which ever was on the steer he would get him by the horns, then fall off in front of the steer, grab his nose with his teeth, and give him a twist and down he fell and on top of the steer. The last I heard of these boys, was only a few years ago. They were with some rodeo and still giving a few exhibitions.

West Darlington, was the Clown of the show, he had a small Shetland pony that he had trained to do all kinds of tricks. He had the pony covered with cow hides, so this is about as I remember the First Taylor Fair.

In the 1890's, Bill and his brothers organized the Pickett Brothers Bronco Busters and Rough Riders

A page from the advertisement of the Pickett Brothers Broncho Busters and Rough Riders Association, which operated in Taylor, Texas prior to 1900.

Association with the following officers: B. W. Pickett, president; W. M. Pickett, vice president; J. J. Pickett, treasurer; B. F. Pickett, secretary; and C. H. Pickett, general manager. They advertised in their handbills: "We ride and break all wild horses with much care. Good treatment to all animals. Perfect satisfaction guaranteed. Catching and taming wild cattle a specialty." They operated several years and had many satisfied customers in the Taylor area.

The late W. Angie Smith, Methodist bishop of Oklahoma for nearly a quarter of a century, was born in Texas and recalls his boyhood:

I was a boy in Taylor and Bill Pickett would return to his home for a visit. He was a real celebrity in the town when he was there. As I recall his style of bull throwing was to leave his horse, grab the bull and sink his teeth in the lip of the bull and throw him that way. Maybe there are others who have used that method but he was the first and so far as I know the last.

Dr. J. Gordon Bryson, a native of Texas and Williamson County who practiced medicine for a life time at Bastrop, was well acquainted with the Picketts and their history:

Yes, the Pickett brothers descended from slaves brought into this community by the Bartons . . . from South Carolina during the mid or late 1850's.

"Tis a happy moment, indeed, when someone comes forward to substantiate a factual, but wild-sounding, statement which has slipped out in an enthusiastic declaration. Right now I am thinking about Will Pickett, who threw and dragged the big steer with his teeth. . . . I saw him at a county fair in Florence, Texas. He was the star of the rodeo team, in 1903.

Well, Clarence Digglingham not only said he saw it at the Florence Fair on the same day I did, but he brought out a copy of June 21 *Grit* with an article by Glen Shirley telling about Will Pickett. Will was referred to as a half-breed, and it was not made clear he was a Negro (in the United States any person with at least 1/16 Negro blood was regarded as a Negro) born on South Gabriel (river) near Liberty Hill. In early Texas history, the term half-breed indicated Indian crossing.

He joined the famous Miller Brothers Wild West Show. Writers have placed him in the "hero role" in magazines. Just where fiction begins and fact ends, I don't know.

Available evidence seems conclusive that in 1898, Willie M. Pickett was a private in the Taylor company of the National Guard, designated first as the Texas Volunteer Guards and later as the Taylor Rifles. He had a blue uniform with a blue cap and wore an insignia of two brass guns. Captain G. Mandell Booth organized the 100-man company in 1891. He was commander, and Tom Jones was first lieutenant. The armory was two blocks from Booth's bank, and many social functions were held there.

For two weeks each year, members of the Taylor Rifles trained with other Texans at Austin's Camp Mabry. Here they ranked high among the five thousand assembled guardsmen. A great disappointment to the men was the fact that during the Spanish-American War when they asked to go into battle, they were rejected in favor of the Georgetown cavalry unit. The only remaining memorial to the Taylor Rifles is a beautiful stained-glass window in the First Christian Church at 603 Talbot Street in Taylor. It was donated and installed by the company in the early 1890's and bears an inscription to that effect.

Lee Moore of Rockdale, Texas, who managed Bill Pickett's first public exhibitions of bulldogging at the turn of the century.

↳ III ↲

PICKETT GOES
PROFESSIONAL

Lee Moore, who ranched near Rockdale, was said to have been involved in the Wyoming cattle wars before he moved to Texas. Bill Pickett had worked for him off and on for a number of years when Moore decided to take Bill to county fairs and gatherings of cowmen and let him bulldog steers with his teeth. There would be an admission fee, of course, and Bill would receive a small percentage for doing most of the work. Bill consented, and under Moore's management, he bulldogged at various events in Houston, Fort Worth, Taylor, Dublin, San Angelo, and most of the other cow towns in Texas. He never failed to receive great applause when he dogged a steer with his teeth.

It was time to branch out, so Moore began to book Pickett in other states. In 1900, Bill and his brothers appeared at the Arkansas Valley Fair in Rocky Ford, Colorado, where Bill gave the first exhibition of public bulldogging in the state. For the next two years, he dogged in Arizona, Texas, Colorado, and several other ranching states.

After the 1902 season, Moore and Pickett dissolved their working agreement. Early in 1903, Pickett teamed up with widely known cowboy and promoter Dave McClure, who booked him at rodeos all over the country, including Phoenix, Tucson, and Prescott, Arizona. This was the beginning of much public notice of Bill's bulldogging stunt, and from Arizona, he and McClure moved to a fair at Grand Forks, North Dakota.

Pickett's new manager was known among rodeo people as Mr. Cowboy, and because he was gifted in his chosen field, he did much to establish Pickett as a great western attraction, billing him in newspapers and show programs as Will Pickett, the most daring cowboy alive, the Dusky Demon. He was wise enough not to identify Pickett as a Negro because during Pickett's life, at most contests, Negroes were automatically barred from competition because most whites felt that it was below their dignity to compete with a black man, even if he carried more than one-half Indian and white blood in his veins. By this time, however, Pickett was a tremendous success and a great attraction at any kind of a gathering: he was the only professional bulldogger in the world.

Pickett created quite a stir at the 1904 Cheyenne Frontier Days celebration, held August 30 through September 1 (Tuesday through Thursday) at Frontier Park. *The Wyoming Tribune* had this to say:

> The event par excellence of the celebration this year is the great feat of Will Pickett, a Negro who hails from Taylor, Texas.

He gives his exhibition this afternoon and twenty thousand people will watch with wonder and admiration a mere man, unarmed and without a device or appliance of any kind, attack a fiery, wild-eyed and powerful steer, dash under the broad breast of the great brute, turn and sink his strong ivory teeth into the upper lip of the animal and, throwing his shoulder against the neck of the steer, strain and twist until the animal, with its head drawn one way under the controlling influence of those merciless teeth and its body forced another, until the brute, under the strain of slowly bending neck, quivered, trembled and then sank to the ground, conquered by a trick. A trick perhaps, but one of the most startling and sensational exhibitions ever seen at a place where daring and thrilling feats are commonplace.

Pickett is not a big man but is built like an athlete and his feat will undoubtedly be one of the great features of this year's celebration. It is difficult to conceive how a man could throw a powerful steer with his hands unaided by rope or a contrivance of some kind and yet Pickett accomplishes this seemingly impossible task with only his teeth.

The *Denver Post* ran the following account on Tuesday and Wednesday:

FOR BRONCHO BUSTING AND STEER THROWING UNEQUALED—Ira Wines and Will Pickett, Who Will Give Exhibition at Cheyenne, Are the Best in the World at Their Specialties.

Of all the features of the celebration, Will Pickett, the colored man who throws steers with his teeth, will perhaps be the most novel.

"Ropes is all right for to hang people wif, but dey gets in de way when ya' wants to rope a steer." This is the paradoxical declaration of Pickett, the Dusky Demon of the Cow Ranch.

The ivory adornments of that spacious opening in the colored man's face attest to the truthfulness of every word he uttered, for the teeth that remain are big and sharp and strong, but several are gone in part as the result of encounters with es-

41

pecially muscular steers, which refused to be humbled without a struggle.

Goes on to Explain

"Yessah. Ah t'rows dem wif mah teeth," he declared, when the young man to whom he was talking began to look wild-eyed and anxious.

"Ah's tellin' yo' de truf-shore." And then he went on to explain just how he caught, threw and tied a steer in 12 1/2 seconds without the use of a lariat, beating the world's record with a lariat by 5 1/2 seconds.

"De rope's jes' in the way," he persisted. "Yo' see, Ah jes' gets mah hos' an' dey turns de steer loose an' Ah goes to 'im jes' like Ah has a rope an' w'en Ah comes up to his head Ah jumps offer de hos' an' nails de steer by de horns—mah lef' hand 'cross his neck lights on his lef' horn, an' mah right hand grabs de right horn. Den Ah pulls up his head an' stops his running—den Ah reaches over de top of his head wif mah own head an' grabs 'im by de upper lip wif mah teeth—what's left of 'em—an t'rows mahself back mighty hard, an' de steer he kirflollops on de groun'—sometimes he lights on me—sometimes he doesn't, but, anyhow, Ah hol's 'im till Ah ties his feet." And the Dusky Demon peeled his lips back over the white teeth that are left and volunteered no further proof of his prowess.

Does What He Says

As a matter of fact, Pickett does exactly what he says, and has been doing so for several years.

"Ah sees a dog throw a cow," he said, when someone ventured a little flattery on the originality of his performance, "an' dat's wha' Ah gets mah idea."

He is booked for Cheyenne August 30 and 31.

Cheyenne, Wyo., Aug. 31. This is the day. . . .

Cheyenne today has a population of 30,000 and more are coming on every train. . . .

Threw Steer with Teeth

To pick out the best feature of yesterday afternoon's events is quite impossible, for every number on the program was good. But if there is special mention to be made William Pickett,

Bill Pickett grabs a steer with his teeth. Cananea, Mexico, 1906.

the Texas Negro cowboy, who twice threw unaided a wild steer with his teeth, is deserving of it. Pickett's feat was stranger and far greater than the fight of Ursus with the bull, so vividly pictured in "Quo Vadis." He loped down the home stretch mounted on a horse and caught up with the steer that had been turned loose a little in advance of his start. There were many in the audience who thought that it would be impossible for a man to throw a steer with his teeth and the interest became intense. The silence of expectation which settled over the grandstand as the horse drew near the lumbering brute, deepened to a dead calm as the Negro's horse dashed alongside the animal, catching the stride of the steer, and then the Negro leaped from his horse to the steer's back. Pickett wound himself around the animal's neck and fastened his teeth in its upper lip.

Then, with a series of quick jerking movements, the Negro forced the steer to its knees, then it rolled over on its side. The immense crowd cheered the pluckey colored man to the echo, and he again jumped on the back of the steer, which in the meantime regained its feet, and repeated the performance.

New York's *Harper's Weekly* was so taken with the goings-on at Cheyenne that it sent special reporter John Dicks Howe to cover the celebration for the magazine. Here is part of his story:

A Cowboy Carnival in Wyoming
Celebrating Frontier Day in Cheyenne

The events took place at the fair grounds, a mile north of Cheyenne. Near the west end of the arena were constructed huge, powerful corrals, or stockades, in which were imprisoned the wild horses and steers that were to take part in the contests. Running south from the corrals a strong built fence extended towards the center of the oval that running steers or wild horses would take the proper course when their turn came. Back of this fence congregated hundreds of cowboys

Bill Pickett throws up his hands to signal he is the victor. Cananea, Mexico, 1906.

and cowgirls, who acted as aids and assistants in carrying out the various features of the programme. In the stands reserved for guests were noticed the faces of many prominent men of the West, leading railroad officials, the proprietors of the great Denver dailies, and scores of other notables.

The great event of the celebration this year was the remarkable feat of Will Pickett, a Negro hailing from Taylor, Texas, who gave his exhibition while 20,000 people watched with wonder and admiration a mere man, unarmed and without a device or appliance of any kind, attack a fiery, wild-eyed, and powerful steer and throw it by his teeth. With the aid of a helper, Pickett chased the steer until he was in front of the grand stand. Then he jumped from the saddle and landed on the back of the animal, grasped its horns, and brought it to a stop within a dozen feet. By a remarkable display of strength he twisted the steer's head until its nose pointed straight into the air, the animal bellowing with pain and its tongue protruding in its effort to secure air. Again and again the Negro was jerked from his feet and tossed into the air, but his grip on the horns never once loosened, and the steer failed in its efforts to gore him. Cowboys with their lariats rushed to Pickett's assistance but the action of the combat was too rapid for them. Before help could be given, Pickett, who had forced the steer's nose into the mud and shut off its wind, slipped, and was tossed aside like a piece of paper. There was a scattering of cowboys as he jumped to his feet and ran for his horse. Taking the saddle without touching the stirrup, he ran the steer to a point opposite the judges stand, again jumped on its back, and threw it. Twice was the Negro lifted from his feet, but he held on with the tenacity of a bulldog. Suddenly Pickett dropped the steer's head and grasped the upper lip of the animal with his teeth, threw his arms wide apart to show that he was not using his hands, and sank slowly upon his back. The steer lost its footing and rolled upon its back, completely covering the Negro's body with its own. The crowd was speechless with horror, many believing that the Negro had been crushed: but a second later the steer rolled to its other side, and Pickett arose uninjured, bowing and smiling. So great was the applause that the darkey again attacked the steer, which had staggered to its feet, and again threw it after a desperate struggle.

Early in 1904, Frank Greer, publisher of the *Guthrie Daily Leader* in Oklahoma Territory, expressed his desire that the National Editors Association's 1905 convention be held in Guthrie. In discussing the matter with Joe Miller of the 101 Ranch, Greer remarked that bringing the convention to Guthrie would take some doing and he couldn't see that Guthrie had much to offer as an inducement. "The hell we haven't," said Joe, adding that if he were given a little time to collect a hundred or so cowboys and cowgirls, he could put on a show second to nothing the editors had ever seen before. The convention was as good as scheduled because when the Millers got behind something, they pushed it to success.

George W. Miller, father of the three Miller brothers of 101 Ranch and 101 Ranch Wild West Show fame, was a Confederate veteran from Crab Orchard, Lincoln County, Kentucky. He was born on February 22, 1841. After his father died, he was reared by his grandfather, John Fish. During the Civil War, he traded in mules and was able to purchase a portion of his grandfather's plantation. Soon after that, on January 9, 1866, he married Mary Ann "Molly" Carson and settled down to the business of rearing a family, farming, and raising cattle. His first son, Joseph Carson Miller, was born on March 12, 1868.

Colonel Miller became dissatisfied with his lot in Kentucky, sold his holdings, and moved to Newtonia, Missouri, where he began his ranching in earnest. He trailed his first herd of Longhorns up from Texas in 1871, and continued in this type of operation until 1893. His second child, a girl christened Alma, was born in Newtonia on June 21, 1875. A second son was born on April 26, 1878. His name was Zachary Taylor Miller, and he was to become the showman of the sons. Meanwhile, George Miller sold out for a second

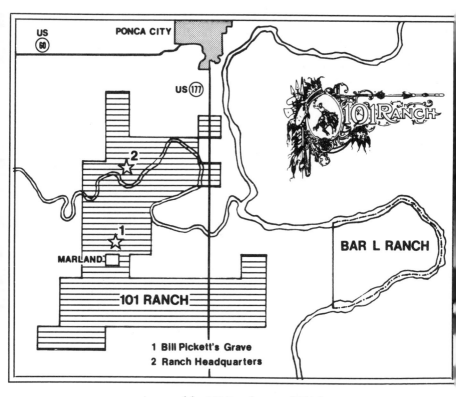

A map of the 101 Ranch area of Oklahoma.

time and moved his family and possessions to Baxter Springs, Kansas, where the third son, George Lee Miller, was born on September 9, 1891.

When it became unprofitable to trail Texas cattle to the railheads in Kansas, Miller shifted to a more diversified operation. He introduced better beef breeds (Shorthorn and Hereford), added swine and poultry, and raised wheat, corn, and alfalfa. It was the bud of an idea that burst into full bloom as one of Oklahoma's most widely known ranches: the 101.

The first headquarters of the 101 Ranch was a semi-dugout on the south bank of the Salt Fork of the Arkansas River in the Cherokee Strip in what is now Kay County, Oklahoma. The White House, a well-known landmark and permanent headquarters for the 101, was completed on the north bank in the fall of 1903. However, George W. Miller, did not live to enjoy it. He died on April 25, 1903, of pneumonia, contracted as he walked in a cold rain from the railroad station in Bliss (now Marland) out to the ranch headquarters. The operation of the ranch fell into the hands of Molly Miller and her three sons.

The Miller Brothers 101 Ranch grew until it contained 110,000 acres of land in present-day Kay and Noble counties. Three towns lay within its boundaries: White Eagle, Red Rock, and Bliss. It could boast of 25,000 head of cattle, 250 employees, 100 head of saddle horses for everyday use, telephone service (35 miles of wire) to all foremen, and daily mail service to all points on the ranch. Schools and churches and miles of roads. A refinery turned home crude into gasoline, fuel oil, and kerosene for ranch use. The ranch had a restaurant, community store, packing-house and cold-storage plant, cider mill, alfalfa mill, modern dairy, and poultry-processing plant. There was also a tannery, as well as a saddle and harness shop, a canning factory, and electric generating plant, a laundry, and a newspaper press. The ranch had its own zoo, the largest herd of buffalo in the world, all types of stallions from Arabians to Percherons, the world's biggest herd of Duroc-Jersey hogs, and the largest herds of Hereford, Shorthorn, and Holstein cattle in America.

George W. Miller's association with the 101 brand was initiated in 1879 when he leased sixty thousand acres from the federal government; however, the brand was not used until 1881. The land, located in the Cherokee strip, provided room for increased cattle-raising activities and helped launch Miller into big-time ranching. In 1881, he moved his family to Winfield, Kansas, to be closer to his ranching operations. He began to brand *101* on the left horn of his cattle, which also carried a large *NO* on the left side and the brand *JK* on the left shoulder. Several other brands and marks accumulated by Miller were used on both horses and cattle until 1888, when the horn brand was eliminated and all animals were branded *101* on the left hip. The *NO* and the *JK* were discarded at this time, and other markings also were discontinued.

There are many stories about the origin of the 101 brand, used by a number of outfits before and after the Millers. A Texas cowman named Doss used it before 1880, and he and two other Texas cattlemen operating a ranch at Kenton, Oklahoma, used it. The Western Land and Cattle Company, Ltd., of London, England, bought the ranch at Kenton and operated it for a number of years. The 101 brand also was used in Wyoming and Nebraska by other cattle out-fits and is still in use on several Oklahoma ranches today.

Some say the Millers bought the brand from the

Western Land and Cattle Company, which seems unlikely because the Kenton ranch was still operating when George W. Miller began to use the brand in 1881. Another story is that the Miller ranch contained 101,000 acres, but the colonel was ranching only 60,000 acres in 1881. A third suggestion is that George W. Miller bought out a small outfit with the brand -0- and because it was hard to read from a horse, he tilted the bars upright and had *101*. The ranch was approximately 101 miles from Oklahoma City, 101 miles from Tulsa, and 101 miles from Wichita—another reason for the name.

Perhaps the most bizarre explanation is that the 101 was named after a sporting house in San Antonio. The story goes that George W. Miller's trail hands had a big fight in a sporting house called the 101 and had to pay for the damage. He told them he would use 101 as a brand on the trail herd to remind them to stay out of trouble.

The most practical deduction was put forth by one of the old 101 Ranch cowboys, Milt Hinkle. He said the brand was adopted so that the ranch cowboys could rework the federal government's ID brand, which was used on Indian agency cattle. It was possible to add *I* and have a very passable *101* or just blot the brand by running *101* over *ID*. Milt confessed that he had performed this little piece of art on many occasions, as had Bill Pickett.

Whatever its origin, the 101 brand became a world symbol of all that was great in a western cattle ranch and remained so for more than forty years. Referred to by many as the fabulous 101, the ranch was without

The 101 Ranch General Office, Store and Meat Market as it appeared in 1975. It looks much the same in this photograph as it did fifty years earlier.

equal in the West, so much so that during a single year, more than one hundred thousand people from all over the world were listed in its guest book. They found the Millers to be a rugged breed in a turbulent time when only the hardiest survived.

Frank Greer attended the 1904 National Editors Association convention in St. Louis, accompanied by Joe Miller and a number of other persons interested in bringing the 1905 meeting to Oklahoma Territory.

Greer promised his fellow journalists good facilities in Guthrie and one of the greatest wild west shows ever seen in the West. Guthrie got the nod. The convention was scheduled for June 7, 8, and 9.

Says Frederick Melton ("Foghorn") Clancy, one of the rodeo's finest announcers: "The first time I ever saw a steer bulldogged was at Dublin, Texas, in 1905 by Bill Pickett. This was at an old settlers reunion with a roping and riding contest as the main attraction." Sometime in May of that year, Bill bulldogged at a Phoenix rodeo attended by C. M. Davis of Fort Worth. From Phoenix, circumstances would lead Pickett to a performance in Fort Worth and, eventually, a commitment to bulldog at the 101 Ranch.

When he returned from St. Louis, Joe Miller conferred with his two brothers, Zack and George, and the three decided they would have to begin immediately to gather up a few additional cowboys with specialties of their own to spice up the big show for the editors. Joe had heard various stories about a Texas cowboy named Bill Pickett who was said to be the only professional bulldogger in the world. Especially intriguing, observers said, was Pickett's bite-'em hold. This all sounded good to Joe, so he sent Zack to Fort Worth to see Bill Pickett perform his incredible feat.

Many men have contributed much to the development of modern rodeo, but the one who probably did more than any other to promote genuine contests was Guy ("Cheyenne Bill") Weadick of the province of Alberta, Canada, where he was a working cowboy and rancher. Until 1912, the only three worth-while annual contests were at Pendleton, Cheyenne, and

Prescott; at none of these did the purse and the money paid for contracted exhibition acts exceed four thousand dollars. Weadick startled the West in 1912 by putting up twenty thousand dollars in prize money at the Calgary Stampede. He was first to offer big-money prizes to attract top competitors from all over the West, a venture in which he was joined by western movie star Tom Mix. Four years later, in 1916, Weadick brought the East its first cowboy contest: he arranged a rodeo in New York City.

In 1905, Weadick teamed up with Bill Pickett as his manager and traveling companion. Pickett was on the program of the Fort Worth Fat Stock Show that year, billed to bulldog bite-'em style. The event was held in a corral on the bank of Marine Creek. After watching Bill bulldog two steers, Zack Miller asked him and Weadick to appear under the 101 Ranch banner as a featured attraction during the editors convention. Pickett was agreeable and promised to come up to the ranch early so that he might practice a little before the great day.

June 11, 1905, dawned bright and balmy on the prairie as 30 regular and special trains—some double headers and all loaded to the gills, with some passengers riding on the top of the cars—deposited 65,000 men and women at the 110,000-acre 101 Ranch to view the Miller Brothers' Big Round-Up (sometimes referred to as the Great Buffalo Chase). The largest crowd ever assembled in Oklahoma Territory up to this time was on hand.

The arena and grandstand were directly east across the section line from the ranch house and the ranch store. At 2:00 P.M., the parade, nearly a mile long, began to make its entry from the east, passed in front of the grandstand, and went out the east gate of the large pasture fenced off for the occasion. Leading the parade, riding abreast, were the three Miller brothers: Joe C., the farmer; Zack T., the rancher and showman; and George L., the financier. The Oklahoma Territory National Guard Cavalry Band, a number of whose members had appeared in the parade with the Mull-hall Cowboy Band at the inauguration of President Theodore Roosevelt on March 4, came next, followed by Geronimo, the bandy-legged little Apache chief who for years outwitted the armies of both Mexico and the United States in a last-stand fight against civilization, pillaging and murdering on both sides of the border. He was old and wrinkled now, officially a prisoner at Fort Sill. Joe Miller had the idea to let people at this roundup see him kill his last buffalo before he died. Geronimo was followed by more than two hundred Indians from the Ponca, Oto, Missouri, Tonkawa, Pawnee, Kaw, and Osage tribes.

Following close behind the Indians was a long procession of cowboys and cowgirls, including Bill Pickett (at the 101, Pickett was always called Bill rather than Will, as he was known to many elsewhere), Guy Weadick, Sam Garrett, Tom Mix, Milt Hinkle, Henry and Tom Grammer, Charley Mulhall, Johnny Brewer, Jim Hopkins, and Lucille Mulhall on her trained horse Governor (Lucille became known as America's First Cowgirl). Indians wearing war paint and armed with lance and bow came next, followed by homesteaders in covered wagons drawn by oxen.

Tom Mix as he looked when he was employed on the 101 Ranch and appeared with the 101 Ranch Wild West Show. Bill Pickett and Mix were good friends and worked together over the years.

Noteworthy in the parade were several men, among them Sam Garrett, who served as grand marshal of many well-known western rodeos and won the All Around Cowboy title in 1914 at Fall Brook, California, and the Pendleton Round-Up. He is the only man ever to win the title of World Champion Trick Roper seven times at the Cheyenne Frontier Days.

At one time, Tom Mix was arena director for the Miller Brothers' 101 Ranch Wild West Show. He later went to Hollywood, where he starred in 370 western movies and earned more than six million dollars as the most widely known and most successful of the silent-movie cowboys. He appeared with the Sells-Floto Circus for three seasons as star of the Wild West After Show and was considered the biggest attraction in the circus world. In 1934, Mix bought an interest in a circus and added his own stables and equipment to the show, known as the Sam B. Dill Circus and Tom Mix Wild Wild West Show. After the first season, Mix acquired sole ownership and the show was billed as the Tom Mix Circus and Wild West. On October 12, 1940, five wives later and broke, Tom Mix was killed in an automobile accident near Florence, Arizona. He died as he had lived: glamorously, with his boots on, at ninety miles per hour behind the wheel of his beloved Cord in the country he made famous on film. The state of Arizona erected a monument at the site of the accident, eighteen miles south of Florence on U.S. 80.

Charley Mulhall, son of Colonel Zack Mulhall and brother of Lucille, was billed with his father's wild west show as Champion Bronc Buster of America. He was a close friend of Tom Mix.

The Millers had picked fine talent for the show: Johnny Brewer was a top hand and could ride the saltiest of broncs. Jim Hopkins was a roper par excellence (once, dead drunk, he won a five-hundred-dollar steer-roping bet using a loop and casting style he had never tried before). Henry Grammer was one of the greatest steer ropers of all times and a very good bronc rider. Joe Miller would bet you any amount you wished to name that Henry Grammer could ride a wild bronc with a half-dollar under each boot in the stirrup and would not lose either coin during the ride. In later life, Henry was a judge at many large rodeos. Tom Grammer, Henry's brother, was regarded as a fine all-around cowboy, but not in a class with Henry.

The first event on the 101 Ranch program for June 11, 1905, was a buffalo hunt by the Indians, painted and dressed in all of their finery. In this act, Geronimo did indeed kill his last buffalo (it was barbecued and served to the editors as a special treat). Then came bronc riding and Indian ball (stickball). Lucille Mulhall performed next, followed by Bill Pickett's bulldogging, the roping contest, and an Indian war dance and powwow. The grand finale was an Indian raid on a wagon train.

Lucille Mulhall and Governor received noisy acclaim from the crowd. She rode Governor down the arena in front of the grandstand at full speed, then, leaning far over in the saddle, picked up a blue kerchief from the ground. Lucille later was recognized as World Champion Woman Roper and was one of the few women who roped steers competitively with men. Oklahoma humorist Will Rogers, her friend and teacher, called her the world's greatest rider.

The most thrilling event of the day was announced by Guy Weadick: "Ladies and Gentlemen, the next event will be Bill Pickett, the Dusky Demon from Texas, who will leap from the back of a running horse onto a running steer and throw the steer with his bare hands and teeth." A one-thousand-pound steer moving at full speed appeared first, followed closely by a mounted hazer whose job was to keep the steer running straight and in front of the grandstand. Next appeared Bill Pickett on his bay war horse, Spradley, as the steer reached a point fifty feet ahead of him. Pickett was in his prime, a man of thirty-three with the energy of a man of twenty, dusky coloring revealing both his Cherokee and Caucasian ancestry. He stood five feet seven inches, weighed 145 pounds, and was as hard and tough as whalebone, with a thin waist and legs and powerful shoulders and arms. He wore a short moustache and was dressed as a Spanish bullfighter.

Pickett urged Spradley on until he was even with the running steer and on the steer's right side. (At that time, bulldoggers jumped to the left rather than the right, as they do today, because cow ponies were trained to be mounted from the left side; it was also customary to dismount on the left side. Thus it was practical to dog to the left, since horses were trained to expect such procedures.) Then he piled off onto the big steer's back and grasped a horn in each of his strong hands, dug his heels into the ground to slow the steer, and began to twist its neck in order to turn

59

its nose upward. When he was able to reach the nose, he sank his strong white teeth into the steer's tender upper lip, turned loose with both hands, and gave his body a twist. The steer fell over on its side and lay still as Pickett held it bite-'em style. The crowd rose to its feet and rendered very enthusiastic applause—in fact, the best of the day.

The Indian attack on the wagon train was an awesome sight that chilled the blood of many a visitor from the East. It wasn't as easy as it looked, either. Skill and coordination were required of every participant to avoid accidents, injuries, and possible death in making the scene realistic. Even so, there were mishaps now and then in such events. This day, there was none.

Cowboys at the 101 Ranch explained how Pickett acquired and trained Spradley. The fractious colt jumped out of a corral one day and a splinter from the top rail lodged in his brisket. The injury went unnoticed for some time, and a large tumor formed around the splinter. The cowboys thought Spradley was ruined for life because he could hardly walk; in fact, they thought he would have to be destroyed. Pickett saw the colt and took a fancy to him. He secured permission to operate on the colt, and, with the aid of several other cowboys, he removed the splinter and as much of the tumor as he could, then sutured the wound. Spradley received Pickett's constant care for several weeks and finally recovered. Pickett claimed the colt as his own and carefully broke him for use as a bulldogging horse; he was probably the best dogging horse Pickett ever used and was a special favorite with Bill. Spradley's name was derived from his peculiar gait. Pickett claimed Spradley ran with all four feet off the ground at one time and that it was necessary for him to spread his hind legs wider than normal in order that they might pass the front legs without striking them.

The day after the show, George Miller arranged for some movie shots of the ranch and wanted a cowboy to ride a horse over the high south bluff of the Salt Fork of the Arkansas (just east of the present bridge on U.S. 77) and into the flood-swollen stream. There were no takers until Tom Mix heard about the stunt and offered his services. He blindfolded his horse, rode south away from the bluff forty or fifty yards, wheeled, rode off the bluff into the river, and swam the horse over to the north bank. While all of this was going on, the camera operator cranked away, recording Tom Mix's first movie. Hence Tom appeared on film long before William S. Hart and only shortly after the first western star, G. M. Anderson (Broncho Billy). Tom had the longest run of them all. Bill Pickett and Guy Weadick watched the filming; Pickett and Mix became close friends.

Through the years, various companies visited the 101 to make movies about the West and ranch life. *Trail Dust, On With the Show* and *Settling Up the Strip* were filmed on the 101. Part of *North of 36* was filmed there, as were many other motion pictures of that era. Western movie stars who worked for the 101 included Mix, Buck Jones, and Hoot Gibson, all three of whom appeared with the 101 Ranch Wild West Show, as did Tex Cooper, the last of the old scouts. Mix was charged with horse stealing in 1908 while he was working for the Miller brothers. The animal, named Bologny, was a spotted gelding with a 101 brand on the left hip and was valued at seventy-five dollars. The case did not come to trial until July 30, 1934, at which time it was dismissed for want of prosecution by the Millers.

On July 5, 6, and 7, 1905, Guy Weadick presented Bill Pickett to Canadians at the Calgary Stampede. Bill was decked out in gold-trimmed toreador pants and the black silk stockings of a Spanish bullfighter. Grant MacEwan describes him in *John Ware's Cow Country*:

> The performing cowboy rode a fast horse, leaped and seized the steer's horns and twisted the head in such a way as to upset the animal. Then, gripping the steer's upper lip in his own teeth and hanging on bulldog fashion, he'd throw both hands in the air. All the while, the inimitable Guy Weadick, talking in the manner of a circus salesman through a megaphone, made this performance sound like the greatest show on earth.

The *Calgary Herald* carried the following story:

> Will Pickett the Texas Negro cowboy, the originator of steer bulldogging, presented at the Calgary Fair the first exhibition of steer bulldogging ever seen outside of Texas, Oklahoma, New Mexico, and Arizona (Colorado and Wyoming). Pickett's stunt was a feature of the Calgary Exhibition. . . . Pickett, Weadick and a half dozen cowboys left Calgary for Winnipeg to present riding and bulldogging exhibitions. While there, their cattle and horses were stolen, as well as their saddles, chaps, and outfits.
>
> The thieves sold the cattle but trailed the horses south across the boundary line without making formal entry. They were captured in North Dakota, and all stock and equipment sold

by U.S. Customs at public auction after they had been advertised for a certain time. Weadick and Pickett, having lost their outfits in the deal, proceeded south. In Chicago while visiting the Wild West Show and Indian Congress, presented at White City by Col. Fred T. Cummins, Weadick first met the girl he was to marry the following year. She was Miss Flores LaDue. . . . One of the better bronc riders of the day, Harold Mapes, took first place in the bronc riding contest here.

Bill Pickett continued to give bulldogging exhibitions during 1906. He was in San Francisco shortly after the catastrophic earthquake and fire of April 18. He told his family about it when he returned home, and it remained one of his favorite subjects for the rest of his life. His next appearances were in El Paso, Texas, and Cananea, Sonora, Mexico, where he dogged in a rodeo. It has been reported that Pickett bulldogged an elk at the El Paso Fair, and it is quite likely that he did so in 1906 when he was on tour in Mexico, since he was performing at a rodeo just across the Río Grande. The animal was reported to be a male with large sharp antlers that could rip a man in half. It took Bill less than ten minutes to subdue and throw the huge beast, and he walked away without a scratch. As the year waned, Pickett made his way north to the 101 Ranch, where he performed for fifty thousand spectators on September 16. The show commemorated the thirteenth anniversary of the opening of the Cherokee Strip.

Their appetite whetted by the success of the 1905 and 1906 roundups, the Millers were not slow to accept an invitation to the 1907 Jamestown Exposition in Virginia. The appearance was suggested by Presi-

Bill Pickett dogging at Phoenix, Arizona in May, 1905 at the old fair grounds. Dave McClure is the mounted man. Courtesy G. M. Davis.

dent Theodore Roosevelt, and the exposition committee promptly accepted the idea.

The year 1907 was a turning point in the life of Bill Pickett: the Millers signed him to a contract with the 101 Ranch Wild West Show. For years, Joe Miller had cherished a dream of what he would like to do to preserve frontier conditions and customs. Now he had a chance to fulfill it. "Boys ten years old and younger have never seen a genuine wild west show," he said, "and we are going to make it possible for them to see one."

The 101 Ranch Wild West Show opened the 1907 season with its first professional performance on May 2 at the Chicago Coliseum. The crew was made up of 90 cowboys and cowgirls, 70 Indians, and 300 head of horses, buffalo, and Longhorn cattle, as well as rolling stock, such as covered wagons and stagecoaches. The show was handled by the C. W. Rex Company, which also managed the operation at Jamestown. Among the participating cowboys were Bill Pickett, Buffalo Vernon, Lon Seeley, Dan Dix, Vester Pegg, Howard Compton, and George Elser. The program is reproduced on the following pages.

After a two-week run in Chicago, the show moved to Virginia and opened at the Jamestown Exposition on May 20. Lucille Mulhall and Wenona, the champion rifle shot, were added to the program. The 90-minute, 16-act show was featured on the War Path (the amusement section of the exposition) with various other attractions. It was a huge success. In fact, the Millers were so encouraged that they made a hurried trip back to the ranch, put together a second

MILLER BROS.
101 RANCH WILD WEST SHOW
From 101 RANCH
BLISS, OKLAHOMA

En Route to the Jamestown Exposition
Under the Direction of the C. W. REX CO.

COLISEUM, MAY 2 to 15, Inc.

Visit the Indian Camp in the Annex.

PROGRAMME

GRAND ENTRY AT 8:30

INTRODUCTION

Chief Bugler, A. M. Wasser.

Cow Boys from headquarters.

Band of Sioux Indians from Rose Bud Agency.

Bunch of Cow Boys from Cow Skin Camp.

Band of Cheyenne Indians from Cantoment, Okla.

Bunch of Cow Boys from Horse Shoe Bend.

Band of Ponca Indians from Ponca Reservation.

Bunch of Cow Boys from the Dogie Camp.

Band of Arrapaho Indians from Kingfisher, Okla.

Bunch of Broncho Busters from Arizona.

Band of Moki Indians from Arizona.

Horse Ranglers from Bar L Division.

Bunch of Mexican Cow Boys.

Bunch of Oklahoma Cow Girls.

Bill Pickett, the Dusky Demon who throws steers with his teeth.

Chief Bull Bear of the Cheyennes.

Chief Black Elk of the Siouxs.

Eddie Botsford, Chief of all Cow Boys.

Geo. Elser, Horse Breaker and Trick Rider.

Flag Bearer.

Zack Miller, one of the Miller Bros., Manager of the Live Stock Department.

Programme subject to change.

STAGE COACH.—Stage Coach attacked by Band of Hostile Indians and rescued by Bunch of Cow Boys, one of the Cow Boys being killed in the fight. This Coach is a relic preserved by Miller Bros., and now used by them for the transportation of friends and visitors to and from the railroad station.

PONY EXPRESS.—Methods used in transporting Messages to the Frontier in Early Days, now one of the Cow Boy Sports.

INDIAN WAR DANCE.—In Celebration of a Victory.

Ghost Dances and other Indian Dances.

COW BOY SPORTS.—Picking up Objects from the ground from the backs of running horses.

BUFFALO CHASE.—Methods used by the Indians in securing their food in early days. Miller Bros. are the owners of the Finest Herd of Buffalo in existence.

Quadrille on Horseback.

Geo. Elser, Horse Breaker and Trick Rider, showing some of the Cow Boy Sports.

H. Jones catches a wild steer from the back of a running horse without the aid of a rope.

Roping and Riding Wild Long Horn Steers by Cow Boys.

Foot Roping by the Cow Boys.

Rifle Shooting by Cow Boy and Cow Girl (Texana and Reynolds) and Rope Juggling by Fred Burns.

Horse Thief, Showing the Treatment that the Horse Thief receives at the hands of the Cow Boys in the Event of Capture.

High School Horse ridden by Miss Sommerville.

Bucking Horse Riding.

Bertha Ross, Champion Lady Broncho Buster of the World

Bill Pickett, "the Dusky Demon of Texas," a negro, who jumps from the back of a horse going at full speed to that of a steer and then, grappling with the latter, throws it to the ground without using his hands in the operation.

Realistic reproduction of the attack and burning of an Emigrant Train Crossing the Plains.

Finale.

The audience is requested to remain seated until the finale.

The first wagons to cross the plains were the Studebaker, which are used exclusively at the 101 Ranch and in our performances.

show, and shipped it to Brighton Beach, New York, where it set attendance records during a six-week run. The bulldogging chore was handled by Frank Maish and Lon Seeley.

Meanwhile, at the Jamestown Exposition, Lucille Mulhall and Governor set the crowd afire, but the spectacle of spectacles was Bill Pickett on Spradley. Folks stood up and cheered as he bowed. They thought his feat impossible and even after seeing it could scarcely believe their eyes.

Today's rodeo fan would scarcely recognize some of the techniques used by performers at the exposition because so many changes have occurred during the past sixty years. At the turn of the century, both men and women rode bucking horses and steers. Today, broncs and bulls are mounted in chutes and turned loose when the rider is ready to begin his bone-numbing, gut-jarring ride; sixty years ago, chutes were unknown. Steers were bulldogged, ridden, or roped on the run, and a bronc to be ridden was snubbed to another horse in the arena, blindfolded, and saddled. Sometimes it was necessary to ear a bronc down (grab an ear in each hand or, in many cases, simply bite one) in order to subdue it long enough to saddle up. The rider then mounted, the blindfold was jerked off, and the bronc came unwound.

This method not only involved grave risk for the rider, it also posed a threat to the snubbing horse and its rider. Occasionally, a wild and unmanageable bronc would climb right up into the saddle with the snubbing-horse rider. Many a cowboy was kicked, pawed, or jumped on while trying to saddle an outlaw horse.

Another common cause of rodeo accidents was the guy rope. Guy ropes, used to hold up the tenting that covered the seating section, were exposed, and any horse or steer—but particularly those being ridden—that came too close to the outside of the arena might trip and fall over one of them.

Injuries, both severe and superficial, were common in rodeo work, and death was an ever present if unseen visitor. For this reason, the 101 Ranch Wild West Show maintained its own emergency hospital. Each day during the season, from one to six cowboys and cowgirls were temporary patients there as a result of their struggles with four-legged desperadoes. One such incident occurred during the Jamestown Exposition: Bill Pickett was quite seriously hurt while bulldogging one afternoon and was laid up for more than a week. Bill was in no condition to work at the end of that time but would hear of nothing else, so Zack Miller let him rejoin the lineup.

Lon Seeley filled in for Pickett while the Dusky Demon was recuperating, jumping from Spradley onto one of the small lead animals of a four-yoke ox team. James E. ("Curbstone Curby") Smedley, the driver, unyoked the animal and Seeley dogged it. Pickett later told the story that Zack Miller named the animal Old Lon because Seeley would not attempt to throw any of the regular dogging steers.

On October 12, the show closed at the Jamestown Exposition and moved to Richmond, Virginia, for a two-day stand. Its next appearance was at the Georgia State Fair in Atlanta, where it ran for nine days before moving to Louisville, Kentucky, for a seven-day engagement that ended the season. The show arrived at Bliss, Oklahoma Territory, on the morning of November 7. The Miller brothers had no plans to take the show on the road next season, so Bill Pickett packed his war bag and headed for Taylor, Texas, to see his family and spend Christmas at home.

By February 1908, the Millers and Edward Arlington, formerly with Barnum & Bailey Circus and Pawnee Bill's Historic Wild West, had agreed on a joint venture: a wild west show that would travel by rail for the season. Profitably aware of the publicity Bill Pickett had received in 1907, all concerned wanted him back.

So it was that the Miller brothers persuaded Bill to sell out in Taylor, move his family to the 101 Ranch, and become a permanent cowhand there. He was to appear with the show during the season and do ranch work the rest of the year. This arrangement being agreeable, the Picketts moved into two large tents on the ranch in 1908. One of the tents served as a kitchen and dining room, the other as sleeping and living quarters. Later the Millers built the Picketts a two-room house with lean-to a block west of the White House. (Bill's eldest daughter, Nannie Pickett Holmes, furnished much of the material concerning the family's life in Texas and Oklahoma. She was Bill's favorite and conducted much of the family business for him over the years. She was twelve when they moved to the 101.)

When Lucille Mulhall visited the 101 Ranch, she also dropped in on Bill and his family. "Bill is a square shooter," she once said of him, also contending that he had saved her life on many occasions and was the perfect pickup man in riding events at rodeos and wild west shows. The Pickett youngsters undoubtedly looked forward to her visits. There were other interesting happenings, too. For example, Joe Miller counterfeited some of Uncle Sam's money, and at least one of the children can remember having and spending some of it. Joe was sent to a federal penitentiary for his little deception of Uncle, and this is why he would never prosecute anyone. If an employee was disloyal or dishonest, he fired him. He remembered serving his sentence and could never wish such a thing upon any other human being.

The Picketts did not remain long at the ranch. Bill moved his family into a good rented house at 515 Southeast Third Street in Ponca City so that his children might have the advantages of a public-school education. There were only six Negro families in Ponca City at this time, and the board of education set up a school for them in the Methodist church. Many cowboys who knew Bill well were unaware that he had a family because the Picketts no longer lived on the ranch and were seldom seen together. In good weather, Bill would ride the nine miles between the ranch and Ponca City. His wife, Maggie, was apprehensive about his bulldogging and urged him to give it up. However, it was second nature with him, he loved it, and he would not consider quitting, even for a minute.

Bill found a lifelong friend in the drugstore owner at Bliss. His name was Arthur Rynearson, and he did many favors for Pickett through the years. Among those best remembered by Bill was Rynearson's custom of going to the Bliss Cafe, buying a good dinner, and bringing it back to the drugstore for Bill to eat in the back room. It was the only way a Negro could get a hot meal in Bliss at that time.

The 1908 show season began on April 14 at Ponca City, and many of the previous season's performers were on hand: Pickett, Joe and Zack Miller, Floyd Randolph, Johnnie Frantz, Stack Lee, Lon Seeley, Tom Grammer, Tom Mix, William Atterberry, George Hooker, D. V. Tantlinger (most folks called him Vern), Vester Pegg, Oscar Rixson, Charles Tipton, Dan Dix, George Elser, Julia Allen, and Rose Scott. Guy Weadick was added to the roster of cowboys. In all, more than two hundred persons took part in the first performance, and it was exceptionally well attended.

For two weeks, the show played a route through Kansas and Illinois, then returned to Chicago for an extended stay from April 27 through May 9. The next week was made up of one-day stands in Illinois and Iowa, followed by a six-day exhibition in St. Louis. The next two weeks were spent in Missouri and Oklahoma.

It rained almost continuously for the first fifty days on the road. The inclement weather played merry hell with patronage and grounds, as well as morale. Pickett continued to bulldog despite the fact that both his horse and the steers scooted and slipped on the soggy turf. Most of the time it was impossible to determine his color after he had dogged a steer. Fortunately, he escaped injury, but several of the bronc busters were hurt. Julia Allen broke her arm when Old Chain Foot hit the guy ropes; Dan Dix dislocated

Bill Pickett and his brothers after the turn of the century. Bill is on the left.

a shoulder; George Hooker dislocated a hip, fractured two ribs, and suffered internal injuries when a bucking horse fell on him at Howell, Michigan; Charles Tipton and George Elser were hospitalized for various periods.

The second week in June, the show moved north into Iowa, then spent two days in St. Paul and Minneapolis, with St. Cloud and Fergus Falls its final stand before it proceeded into Canada for ten days. Business was very good in Minnesota. The show reopened on June 22 at Winnipeg. On Dominion Day at Calgary, three performances were presented in conjunction with the Dominion Fair. It was Pickett's second appearance in Calgary, and he was given as much acclaim as he got on his first visit. The next stop was Montana, then on to North Dakota. The show was plagued by rain in Montana and had a serious train wreck in North Dakota. However, the tour continued through Wisconsin, Illinois, Michigan, Indiana, Tennessee, Georgia, Alabama, Mississippi, Louisiana, and Texas, the last performance being given at Brownsville, Texas, on December 3. In all, the season was a success, in both experience and financial gain for the Miller brothers.

↳ IV ↲

LONG LIVE THE BULL

Mexico's national sport is bullfighting, and the president of the country is held in no higher regard than the most prominent bullfighters. It has been so since the days of the Conquistadors.

Fighting bulls have been bred as long as and possibly more carefully than beef cattle. The dominant strain seems to have descended from the well-known Miuras of North Africa and was bred by the Egyptians under the Pharaohs. Animals of this stock were brought to Spain about A.D. 1200 by the Phoenicians or other African traders in a semidomesticated state; they reverted in the wilderness of the high Iberian Plateau and finally crossed with the indigenous Aurochs. From this stock, fighting bulls have been bred and culled to give them a small, triangular head; wide, strong horns, which curve forward instead of up; a short neck, with exceptionally heavy muscles, which erects when the bull is angry; wide shoulders; and small hooves.

A fighting bull is all muscle, bone, and horn and has a bred-in love for combat: it is the only reason for his existence. Only exceptional animals are used for breeding stock; those that can't pass the test are sent to slaughter. Fighting bulls are a savage breed. Without the slightest provocation, they will charge anything that affords combat, repeatedly, under all sorts of punishment and with great courage. The nature of the *toro bravo* has changed little over the centuries, and that only in the form of increased viciousness. At the turn of the century, fighting bulls were required to be five years of age (a bull is not fully mature until he is five) and weigh eleven hundred pounds.

In 1526, the Conquistadors staged the Western Hemisphere's first bullfight in Mexico City's main plaza. At about the same time, the first breeding ranch was established at Ateneo with cows and bulls imported from Navarre, Spain. The oldest ranches breeding *toros bravos* are Ateneo at Ateneo in the Province of Mexico, Piedras Negras at Tlaxcala in the province of Tlaxcala, and Santin and San Diego de Los Padres, both near Mexico City. The industry was carried on largely by 8 ranches in one province for many years; today, 135 ranches produce fighting bulls. However, there are only 14 Grade A bull ranches in all of Mexico, and these are considered to be the nation's best. As of 1974, fighting bulls were bringing $600 to $1,000 on the breeding market, and first-class matadors fighting in Mexico were receiving $7,700 or more per fight. The most ever paid a matador for a single fight was the great Manolete's $36,000.

In an atmosphere of medieval pageantry and accompanied by a band playing martial airs, the professional bullfighter uses his skill to provide entertain-ment. Neither he nor his public thinks a bullfight in any way resembles an orgy of senseless butchery and cruelty to a noble animal. The first thing he would make clear to you is that bullfighting is not a sport in the sense that, for example, boxing, football, or base-ball are. Bullfighting is essentially an art rooted deep in human history and is comparable only to a solemn ritual or ballet. If there is a contest, it is within the matador: courage *versus* fear. It is for the Latin a part of his breath of life and is passionately endorsed by his fellow countrymen. They would admit to you that there are elements of cruelty in bullfighting, certainly, but so are there in fox or stag hunting, in obtaining fur for coats, and in the operation of zoological gardens in which shabby animals are condemned to spend years confined in cramped cages until death releases them from the prying eyes of humanity. The Latins' fighting bull spends his first four years of life literally living off the fat of the land and the last fifteen minutes of it in mortal combat. They would also ask you this question: Do any other animals that come into contact with humans have such a high percentage of good luck?

The bullfight is performed on Sunday afternoon at four o'clock sharp in a deep, bowl-shaped stadium known as the *plaza de toros*. A trumpet sounds, and the procession enters the ring, an event that is some-what similar to the grand entry at a rodeo or wild west show. On a standard card, three matadors will fight six bulls. The animals are drawn by name or number

77

on the morning of the fight—just as the bronc rider or bulldogger draws his horses or steers each day at a rodeo.

The bullfight is divided into three acts. Initiating the event are two mounted picadors armed with long, steel spike-tipped lances. Their horses are padded and blindfolded, and the leg of each rider is protected by steel armor. The bull is induced to charge the horses so that the picadors can jab his hump to a depth of two centimeters, thereby reducing the effectiveness of his neck muscles. He will then keep his head down and can be killed in the prescribed manner. After the bull has been lanced, three matadors in succession show what they have to offer in the way of cape work on the now maddened bull. The picadors leave the ring after three strikes of the lance.

The second act features the *banderillero*, who is on foot. He must place three pairs of gaily decorated barbed wooden darts, or *banderillas*, in the bull's shoulders, marking the place where the sword later will be thrust. His action also serves to correct any tendency the animal may have to use one horn more than the other. To place the darts, the *banderillero* usually runs in a half-circle, reaches over the bull's horns, and inserts the darts as his course meets the line of the bull's charge. As is everything else done in the ring, this procedure is intended to tire the bull and prepare it for a formal killing.

The bullfight judge, whose box is located high in the seats on the shady side of the stadium and directly across the ring from the official clock, gives the matador, or *torero*, exactly fifteen minutes to perform, marking the time on a blackboard next to his box. If the bull is not down in ten minutes, the judge signals a trumpeter to sound the first warning. Three minutes later, a second warning is sounded. After fifteen minutes have elapsed, the trumpet is sounded again, whereupon the bullfighter must leave the ring. Trained steers are led in and take the bull out alive. Removal of a live bull from the ring, the epitome of disgrace for a *torero*, is a very rare occurrence in professional fights.

The third and most important act of a bullfight is performed by the matador, armed with a small scarlet cape and razor-sharp sword. He is alone in the ring with the bull, who by this time is somewhat chastened, although still very dangerous and full of fight. The quality of the matador is judged by his proximity to the bull as he works. After a number of passes with the cape and when the matador feels the time is right, he turns sideways, aims his sword over the bull's horns, and plunges the blade between the animal's shoulders. After the kill, the bull is dragged outside the ring by a team of mules and butchered. The meat is sold to the poor at a very nominal price so that nothing is wasted.

When the spectators wave white kerchiefs, they are asking the judge to recognize the *torero* for his cape and sword work. The reward for a good performance is an ear; for an excellent one, both ears; and for a superlative one, the tail also. Very rarely, and only for a perfect bullfight from start to finish, a hoof is given. This has happened once in the Mexico City bullring; the feat was performed by the great Mexican master matador Armillita. In the olden times, there also was a practical purpose in awarding the *torero* an ear; he was paid very little for his performance, and the ear served as a chit with which he could obtain the bull's carcass, as well as earn extra compensation.

During the entire three acts of the performance, the matador will never dare to place even so much as a finger on the bull or in any way grapple with the animal. In fact, provisions are always at hand to avoid personal contact. *Toreros* must preserve themselves through their remarkable courage and their agility in evading the *toro's* furious charges. The scarlet cape waved in front of the bull has been a target for attack since his infancy, not the matador who brandishes it and deftly steps aside. (It is also true that a bull closes his eyes when he charges; a steer does not.) In modern times, the most outstanding matadors of Spain and Mexico have been Juan Belmonte, Rodolfo Gaona, Joselito, Sánchez Mejías, Vicente Pastor, Manolete, and Conchita Cintron.

Juan Belmonte, a short, bowlegged man, was inclined to be sickly. He fought with an air of abstraction and slowness and a pathos that earned him an epithet: Master of Tragedy. In 1919, Belmonte fought 109 bulls in one season, a record that stood until 1950, when Letri fought 115. It is said of Belmonte that he invented what all other bullfighters after him have had to imitate in some way. Certainly he overcame many seemingly insurmountable obstacles in life. He grew up a street urchin in Madrid, and when he saw his brothers and sisters carried off to the poorhouse, he vowed that he would become the greatest and richest bullfighter in the world. While he was very young, he joined a group of hoodlums who also yearned to be *toreros*, and for two years he roamed on ranches at night, fighting dangerous bulls and taking the risk of being shot by guards on patrol. Word spread that he showed much promise, and he was given a chance to prove himself.

Belmonte's only real rival was Joselito (Little Joe), who in 1919-20 was fighting well over a hundred bulls a year, as was Juan. With each fight, Belmonte seemed to do more extraordinary things, and the *aficionados* were paying delightedly to see them. He was the hero of Spain and was widely known in Mexico. His craggy, sorrowful face began to show up everywhere in various kinds of graphic reproductions. His dreams of money, fame, women, and friends came true, yet, at the age of seventy, he took a small pistol from his pocket, held it to his head, and pulled the trigger. He had remarked to a friend the night before: "There are only three things in life I still like to do—make love, ride a horse, and fight bulls,—and my doctor has forbidden me all of them. I should like to die doing one of those things."

Joselito, who amazed the bullfighting world by performing when he was only nine years old, knew everything there was to know about bulls. He was a Gypsy type—tall, dark, graceful—a Spaniard, and both a rival and friend to Belmonte. The last high point of the *corrida de toros* was the period from 1914 to 1920 when he and Belmonte staged their fabulous competition.

Joselito was a picture of perfect domination over the

bull. His style was cold and beautifully classical. Ernest Hemingway says that during the 1914-20 competition, Joselito frequently complained that he worked as close to the bulls as did Belmonte, but because his passes were natural and unrestrained, they didn't look as close. During his sixteen years in the ring, he was gored only twice (both wounds were minor) until the fateful afternoon of May 16, 1920. On that day, he met a treacherous bull named Bailador, and the left horn caught him in the stomach. A few minutes later, he was dead. The nation went into mourning for the 25-year-old hero, and the other bullfighters glanced at each other and said: "God, if they can kill Joselito, what chance have we?"

Sánchez Mejías was Joselito's brother-in-law. He was a brave *torero* and followed closely in the footsteps of Joselito and the other greats. He, too, died in the ring with horns in his abdomen. Manolete, a Spaniard, is considered by many bullfighters to be the greatest *torero* of all times. He is known for his elegant and scientific style. He planned to retire at twenty-nine and live on his ranch and enjoy the several million dollars he had earned by risking his neck since he was thirteen. Then he was challenged by a cocky newcomer named Dominguin. On August 28, 1947, Manolete appeared in Linares, Spain, performing with one of the terrifying Murira bulls, known as the bulls of death. So it happened to him. His helpers lifted him from a pool of his own blood and rushed him to the infirmary, where he died.

Vicente Pastor, one of the early greats who fought in both Spain and Mexico, is best remembered for his performance in Madrid on October 2, 1910. The first ear ever awarded a *torero* in Madrid was presented to Pastor that afternoon. He was one of the few bullfighters who did not spill his lifeblood in the ring. He died in his own bed.

Rodolfo Gaona, known as El Indio, was one of the greatest Mexican bullfighters who ever entered the ring. He was a master of cape, *banderilla*, and sword. The gaonera pass (a special cape maneuver) was named after him. In his late seventies as he awaited his turn to make the last confrontation with death, all who knew him knew he would do so in the same way he faced the bulls: with courage and grace.

Conchita Cintron was a South American beauty. She not only killed bulls on horseback, a Portuguese art, but also fought them on foot, matador style.

The Golden Age of bullfighting in Spain and Mexico began with Belmonte and ended with Joselito's fatal goring in 1920. Nowadays in the *fiesta brava*, there seems to be a lack of *pundonor*, that indefinable combination of pride and honor and guts that once was the essential ingredient in every *torero*. Everything else—skill and grace and good looks—was icing on the cake.

Into such a setting the Miller brothers were to send their wild west show in December 1908. The season in the United States and Canada had been rewarding, and the Millers decided to tour Mexico during the winter. The visit was to include a long engagement in Mexico City.

Many of the show's cowboys, including Bill Pickett, were sent back to the 101 Ranch to take care of the winter chores. There was corn to gather, pecans to harvest, fences to mend, and cattle to feed, along with those endless tasks that must be performed to keep an empire like the 101 running smoothly. It was the ranch's policy to raise feed for and winter twenty-five hundred to four thousand head of cattle and to buy enough additional cattle each spring to eat the surplus grass on the ranges. Under normal conditions, profits from marketing beef cattle fattened on the 101 amounted to thousands of dollars annually.

The ranch had one hundred fine brood mares, and one or more stallions and jacks were kept for breeding purposes and for replenishing the work stock. Huge stables housed the draft horses and mules, and two blacksmiths were kept busy shoeing them and doing other repair work. Hundreds of woven-wire-fenced pens, lots, and fields held thousands of purebred Duroc-Jersey hogs. Income from sales totaled many thousands of dollars each year.

The poultry department was no small thing, either, and its operation required many hands, for it included ostriches, peafowl, turkeys, geese, and pigeons as well as chickens. Modern housing, incubators, and brooders were provided. In poultry, as in everything else, the Millers bred nothing but the best.

The 101's crops consisted mainly of corn and cotton, as well as all kinds of food for the many people who lived on the ranch. The farm work required 450 mules and 300 horses; 100 ponies were used in the cattle business (these figures do not include the horses used in the wild west show).

The diversified multitude of operations on the 101 required a large staff the year round. Most of the show personnel worked on the ranch at various jobs when not on tour. Although everything from common farm stock to buffalo was raised on the Ranch, its principal income-producing animals were cattle, horses, mules, hogs, and poultry. Cattle and hogs were featured every year, and records show that they never failed to yield large revenues.

⛬ V ⛭

THE MEXICAN FIESTA

After completing its 1908 season on December 3 at Brownsville, Texas, the 101 Ranch Wild West Show proceeded to Laredo and on December 5 entered Mexico at Nuevo Laredo, across the Río Grande. Here, customs officials searched the train for guns and ammunition that might be used in the trouble brewing between Francisco Madera and President Porfirio Díaz, who was overthrown by Madera in 1911. Díaz' long rule had created much hardship and heartbreak for the common man in Mexico; in such an atmosphere of fear, then, much suspicion was aroused when a big outfit like the 101 Ranch Wild West Show wanted to cross the border. The customs officers and soldiers pried up the floorboards of the show wagons and looked under them. They opened the ten-gallon lard cans on the cook's wagon and thrust bayonets into the lard to make sure nothing was hidden there. It was a shakedown that left no nook or cranny unexplored.

After clearing customs, the show traveled by rail to Monterrey, where it played on December 6 before moving to San Luis Potosí for two days of shows on the ninth and tenth. On the evening of the eleventh, the show folks staged an illuminated parade on the Paseo de la Reforma in Mexico City. The first performance in Mexico's capital city was held the following day at the circus arena on the Paseo in Porfirio Díaz Park.

Concerned with more serious matters, the people of Mexico City were not patronizing the show to the tune of one thousand dollars a day in losses. The show also had run afoul of some Mexican laws, for which it had been fined, and it was still billed to run for more than two weeks. Mexican law provided a fine of fifty pesos if a show failed to open at the precise hour it was advertised to open, another fifty pesos if the ticket seller sold a single ticket to a patron for whom no seat was available, and fifty pesos more if anyone billed to perform at a show did not appear. In all of its advertising, the 101 Ranch Wild West Show had been listing Bill Pickett's act as part of each performance, while in fact Bill was helping to put up the fall crops at the ranch. In Bill's absence, Vester Pegg had been doing the dogging.

Joe Miller, expert showman that he was, realized that something must be done at once, so he wired his brother George at the ranch to send Pickett to Mexico City on the double. George received the message on or about December 13 and immediately sent for Bill, who was picking cotton for Bailey Carson, a cousin of the Millers (Bill could still pick 500 pounds of cotton a day, which was no small chore in itself).

The night before the message arrived, Pickett dreamed he would receive a wire from Joe Miller telling him to come at once to Mexico City to bulldog. He also dreamed he was being chased by a huge black bull. He told both dreams to Maggie. Bill didn't want to go to Mexico and had decided to say no when asked, but Maggie said to him: "Bill, that's sure enough the Devil after you. You better go to Mexico like your boss says." Bill's answer to George Miller was: "All right, gimme some whiskey and a ticket and I'll go."

Picket boarded the train at Bliss and headed south. His whiskey ran out before he arrived in Guthrie, however, so he got off there and replenished his supply. He got stinking drunk and woke up the next morning penniless and with a splitting headache. There was nothing else to do but wire George Miller for more funds. Miller sent a hundred dollars and also wired Joe to have one of the nondrinking cowboys meet Pickett at Laredo to ensure his safe arrival in Mexico City on schedule. Bill arrived on or about December 16 without further incident and began bulldogging with the show as advertised.

One night, for the lack of anything else to do, a bunch of the show cowboys, including Bill Pickett and Floyd Randolph, decided to visit a bar near the railroad station and siding where the 101 Ranch sleeping cars were spotted. Among the patrons that night were a Negro and a white man, the only Americans Randolph saw during the show's stay in Mexico City. Drinks were one and one-half cents each, and a man and his friends could get drunk on fifty cents. Not long after the arrival of the 101 crew, the Negro made the statement that he was from Texas and he hoped the whole damned state would sink back into the ocean. Pickett took exception to the remark, saying he, too, was from the great sovereign state of Texas and was proud of the fact. A fight started between the two. Pickett knocked the other Negro out, the man falling to the floor in the middle of the room. Everyone in the bar scrambled for the doors because they knew the police would be upon them very soon: there was a policeman stationed on every street corner. The 101 Bunch made their break together; they swarmed over the six-foot steel pickets that separated the station platform from the rails and ran down the tracks to their sleeping cars. They were safely inside and in their bunks when the police arrived at the bar.

Of all the matadors in Mexico and Spain at this time, none was regarded with more respect or received more hero worship than Manuel Majias Bienvenida, also known as Manolo Bienvenida, who was appearing in Mexico City's new concrete-and-steel bull ring, El Toro, the second largest in the world. He was said to be absolutely without fear, noted for his eye, poetic grace, form, and the killing stroke of his blade. There were 465 other matadors in Mexico at this time. Pickett's act in the wild west show was the only one that was comparable to bullfighting in any way, and a group of bullfighters, in the company of Bienvenida, attended a performance one afternoon to see the American Negro dog a steer. They were very much amused by Bill's performance. They laughed with contempt and boasted that they could perform the trick easily and in much less time. The Mexican press also was critical of the show and was especially indignant about Pickett's bulldogging, describing it editorially as disgusting and vulgar and asserting that Pickett lacked the courage, grace, and dignity of a matador.

The rendezvous of the bullfighting fraternity in Mexico City was the Café Colón, which was also frequented by Joe Miller and various reporters from the several newspapers published each day in that city. On the night following the matadors' visit to the 101 show, Joe Miller and his press agent W. C. Thompson, stopped at the restaurant in the hope of getting some much needed publicity from the assembled reporters. The conversation eventually got around to the show and Pickett's bulldogging. Louis F. Correa of the *Mexican Herald* and several bullfighters entered the discussion. The bullfighters were still contemptuous of the show in general and Pickett in particular. Miller was ruffled by their pointed remarks and made his own observations on the merits of Pickett's act. He was fully aware of the skill, agility, and dexterity of matadors in general and particularly of those present, he remarked, but he was of the personal opinion that, for either sport or gold, none of them would be able to make a decent showing in bulldogging a steer because the feat required a special kind of ability and guts. Miller knew the difficulties involved in dogging even for a man who was in the habit of performing once or twice a day. He also knew that the horses used by the bulldogger were more than half the battle because timing and experience were of the utmost importance in dogging a steer. The odds were definitely stacked against the bullfighters.

Bienvenida took immediate exception to Miller's insinuation that the assembled toreadors were lacking in bravery and skill. He accepted Miller's challenge on behalf of the bullfighting fraternity and agreed to bull-dog a steer the next morning at the showgrounds. However, he insisted that the performance be private, attended by invitation only, saying it would be unethical and a disgrace to his profession to make a public spectacle of the affair. He said he would be at the showgrounds promptly at 10:00 A.M. and would give the boasting Americans a lesson in grace, courage, and skill as applied to the subjugation of the bovine species. Miller agreed to Bienvenida's terms, and the die was cast. Correa's *Mexican Herald*, published in English, and *El Heraldo, El Diavio*, the *Mexican Record*, and *El Imparcial*, all published in Spanish, carried the story on the front page of their morning editions. In fact, *El Heraldo* devoted three columns to the event, smugly predicting that Bienvenida would, as promised, "teach the boasting Americans a lesson in courage and grace."

At the appointed hour, several score guests from the press and the show waited and wondered. Bienvenida failed to arrive and sent no word of explanation or apology. Finally, Joe Miller sent a messenger to Bien-venida's hotel for an explanation. Bienvenida was at ease in a comfortable chair. He stated that, regret-fully, he had been forbidden by the authorities of the bull ring, to whom he was under contract, to take bodily risk of any kind, except to fight bulls in the national ring, El Toro.

Miller received the message with mixed emotions. In the presence of reporters from most of Mexico's newspapers, he said it was his personal opinion that

Beinvenida had deliberately shown the coward's white feather. Bienvenida's failure to appear and Miller's remark paved the way for one of the most remarkable contests in the Mexican bull ring.

After thinking it over, Joe Miller decided that opportunity was at last knocking at his door. He would make a new proposal to the bullfighters: he would offer to pit Bill Pickett's dogging against any bull the matadors might choose. It was simply a case of baiting the bullfighters instead of the bull. That night, with Correa, Miller again visited the Café Colón at an hour when most of the matadors were present. To the amazement and chagrin of the assembled toreadors and their admirers, Miller proposed to match Pickett against any fighting bull in all of Mexico that they could ship, lead, or drive into the ring, barehanded and unaided in a bulldogging exhibition, and in addition would wager five thousand pesos on Pickett's ability to accomplish the feat. Up to this point, no one had mentioned the matter in any detail to Pickett.

The folly of such a contest was apparent at once to every Mexican present because in his mind it meant a sure, speedy, and bloody death. This foolhardy American cowboy was unfamiliar with the ferocity and strength of fighting bulls and the practices of the bull ring.

The following morning, December 20, the newspapers carried Miller's offer, repeating his statement that it was not hard to fight a bull and that bullfighters are not necessarily brave. This caused an uproar in Mexico City; it was regarded as an insult to the matadors and the national sport. The papers and people in general considered it a *gringo* bluff and publicly demanded that Pickett and Miller make good on their bravado. They would turn out in force, they agreed, to watch Pickett sacrifice his life to a fighting bull on the altar of American egotism.

Don Jose del Rivero, manager of the bull ring, covered Miller's bet and suggested that the contest be held at El Toro. Miller agreed and invited Rivero to select the bull. The bull ring's staff was to take charge of ticket sales and handle the advertising, as well as secure special permission from Federal District authorities to present the exhibition at El Toro (Mexican law required that permits be obtained from the governor of the Federal District in order to stage bullfights or other large sporting events).

Ground rules were drawn up and agreed upon. Pickett was not to flee from the bull, no matter how fierce or powerful the animal's rushes. He was to fight the bull, rough and tumble, for fifteen minutes unless he succeeded earlier in bulldogging the animal flat on its back. He was to wear his customary red shirt and enter the arena alone, unarmed, and unprotected. Joe Miller was no greenhorn. He knew that a fighting bull, like a buffalo, had a much stronger and more muscular neck than a wild, spooky Texas steer. Therefore, he did not bet that Pickett would definitely bulldog the animal; instead, he insisted that the Dusky Demon would stay with the bull for a full fifteen minutes of turbulent action and would spend at least five minutes grappling with it in mortal hand-to-bull combat. Miller was to receive all of the gate receipts, plus the five-thousand-peso bet, if Pickett were successful. If he failed, Miller would get only funeral expenses.

Permission was granted for the contest, to be held not on Thursday (Christmas Eve), as requested, but on Wednesday, December 23, 1908, at four in the afternoon. Rivero selected a coal-black bull named Bonito to share the honors with Pickett. A year earlier, Bonito had shown himself to be one of the most fearless and destructive bulls ever to enter the ring. By request of the *aficionados*, his life was spared in recognition of his great heart and fearlessness—something that is seldom done.

The Mexican press and promoters of the great exhibition had a heyday. Bienvenida was quoted in the newspapers as predicting that "Pickett's funeral will follow his foolhardiness." Said one headline: "Pickett Will Face Spanish Bull Alone. Negro Rough Rider Will Take Life in Hands. Full Performance at Bull Ring Tomorrow. Authorities Grant License." Another read: "Greatest Sensation in the History of the National Sport of Mexico. Never Before a Man So Brave; Pickett Dusky Demon of Oklahoma." Bloody advertisements were posted on the streets and distributed throughout the city, working the populace up to a frenzied pitch. In fact, members of the bull ring staff were fearful that the Federal District governor would withdraw permission for the event.

When informed of the contest, Bill Pickett was all for it because he believed there was no bull on earth he couldn't stay with fifteen minutes. However, he did extract from Miller a promise that if anything went wrong and he were killed, his remains would be returned to the 101 Ranch and buried there. This was fine with Miller, of course, because he had every confidence in his supercowboy. Pickett was not afraid of the bull or even of being killed, but he was quite apprehensive about being interred in a foreign country. He wanted to be buried among friends in the 101's firm ground, where the coyotes couldn't scratch out his bones.

Pickett paid little attention to the uproar and went about his daily work with an air of self-confidence. In fact, he made plans to attend a dance on the eve of the contest. Joe Miller did not think this was such a good idea, so he selected two of the show's Indians to guard him and checked him into the Hotel St. Francis for a good night's sleep. He wanted Pickett in tiptop shape on the morrow.

The afternoon of the great day finally arrived. At El Toro, a turn-away crowd of more than twenty-five thousand, the largest in the bull ring's history, filled all available seats well over an hour before the show was scheduled to begin. Among the spectators were President Díaz and many other high officials. Gate receipts were reported to be more than forty-eight thousand pesos; this, plus the side bet of five thousand pesos, made a grand total of fifty-three thousand pesos up for grabs.

The 101 Ranch Wild West Show troupe arrived on time without incident and was met by a much surprised Rivero, who later confessed that he did not believe Pickett would have the courage to show up. Bedecked in their outfits, the matadors strutted into the ring in a preperformance parade, carrying an elaborate black coffin upon which was inscribed: *EL PINCHARINO* ("one who has been gored through"). There was no question in the minds of the spectators about the outcome of the contest; it was merely a matter of time. There persists a story that Mexico City bookmakers were giving Pickett only four minutes to live after entering the ring. Thousands of pesos were wagered.

All other parts of the show were to be presented before Bill Pickett tried to bulldog Bonito. The grand parade was run off as usual and the various acts followed in their usual order, but the spectators showed little interest. They had come to see Pickett versus Bonito and soon let it be known, shouting, "El Pincharino! El Picharino! El Pincharino!" The sound in the packed stadium was deafening. Then the unruly crowd began to call for the bull: "Bonito! Viva el toro!" At this point, there came staggering news: the governor of the Federal District had withdrawn permission for Picket to face Bonito.

At noon, a delegation of American women who were living in Mexico City had called on the governor, protesting the contest in the name of humanity and arguing that Pickett would surely be killed. The women had enlisted the influence and assistance of some powerful American businessmen and officials, and the governor couldn't resist. He grudgingly revoked the permission he had granted so gladly.

The officials at El Toro were not ready to give up. They pointed out to the governor that Bonito was the only bull mentioned in the request for cancellation. They also pointed out that there were other bulls, all savage, and that Pickett was willing to meet any one of them. The governor was persuaded to let Rivero select another bull for the contest.

Rivero chose Frijoli Chiquita (Little Beans). Fully as wary, wild, and ferocious as Bonito, this bull came from the world-renowned bull ranch at Tepeyahualco, for years a supplier of outstanding animals. Frijoli Chiquita was a magnificent fighter with an oddly speckled hide that was almost purple in hue. His horns were short and sharp, his neck strong and thick (in fact, he was about three-quarters neck and head with almost no hind quarters). He looked as if he had even greater strength than Bonito. In sum, he was in every respect a most formidable substitute and promised to give Pickett all he could handle.

A huge sign was displayed before the partisan spectators: "By request, Bonito has been withdrawn and another bull substituted." The implication was that Miller or Pickett had made the request, fearing Bonito's reputation and courage. The crowd showed its displeasure with shouts of derision and angry demands for refunds. A second bulletin was posted, explaining that Bonito had been withdrawn by order of the governor of the Federal District and that an equally fierce bull, Frijoli Chiquita, had been selected by Don Jose del Rivero as a substitute. The crowd yelled and hooted during the rest of the wild west show, paying little attention to the acts and shouting, at each intermission, for the black cowboy from Oklahoma and the bull. The show was cut short, and it was announced that the grand event was coming up next.

Zack Miller offered Bill Pickett a bottle of whiskey. Bill drank about a pint, returned the now half-full bottle, put spurs to Spradley, and rode into the bull ring, followed closely by the hazer, Vester Pegg, who was on an excellent horse named Silver. Several other cowboys also rode into the ring, each armed with a .45, to protect Pickett in the event something went wrong.

Spradley, one of the best bulldogging horses in the business, seemed eager for the contest. His bay coat glistened in the evening sun, and every ounce of his nine hundred pounds seemed to be wound tight as a spring as he dashed into the ring. He seemed to understand the urgency of the moment and the needs of his rider.

Pickett was dressed in the typical garb of a working cowhand; a good Stetson hat that once had been white; a colored neckerchief; a red shirt; ducking pants, held up by a wide leather belt fastened with a large silver buckle; and shop-made boots, knee length with square tops.

The Dusky Demon and his colleagues were greeted by boos and cheers as they took their positions near the gate through which the bull was to enter the arena. A trumpet sounded and a gate was thrown open. Frijoli Chiquita, fortified with the courage of more than a hundred generations of killers, came in with a rush and a snort, sighted Pickett and Spradley, and made a wild charge at horse and rider as a mighty shout of approval rose from the crowd. For the first time, Pickett realized just what he was up against. This was no wild and spooky Texas steer that would run away in a straight line; on the contrary, Frijoli Chiquita was bringing the fight to him. W. C. Thompson, publicity man for the 101 show, later reported to U.S. newspapers that Frijoli Chiquita's size and proclivities were as much like those of his bovine American brothers as the same characteristics in a wildcat and a chipmunk. It was also reported that Pickett had never seen a fighting bull before this encounter. However, he was not frightened because he had confidence in both his horse and himself. Cowboys and ranchers who worked with Pickett for years said he was absolutely without fear to his dying day.

Bill was at a disadvantage from the beginning because the hazer could not drive the bull away from him so that Bill could make a proper approach. They tried several times to get the bull into position, with no success. Frijoli Chiquita pressed his attack on man and mount from the moment he entered the ring. The other cowboys had all they could do to prevent the bull from goring their horses. They fired blank cartridges in his face when he attacked them, and this kept them so busy that they were of little use to Bill in his hour of need. Vester Pegg's horse, Silver, was hooked in the flank as Vester attempted to haze the bull away and into position. Finally, from a very awkward position, Bill tried to get a hold on the bull's horns; he failed, narrowly escaping a horrible death. He then rode out of the ring amid the jeers and howls of the bloodthirsty crowd.

Fearful that Spradley would be gored, Pickett asked Joe Miller for another horse. The crowd, thinking Pickett had shown the white feather, began to shout and demand that the contest be completed; they were indeed in an ugly mood and wanted to see Pickett gored. Miller realized that if the contest were not continued at once, it was quite possible that none of the Anglos would leave the bull ring alive. He told Pickett to "get back out there and take that goddamned bull before we are all killed," declaring there was no time to change mounts and that the Mexicans were on the verge of rioting. Pickett and Spradley returned to the ring.

Frijoli Chiquita immediately charged Spradley, who evaded the bull's first mad rush but was unable to avoid the second charge from behind. Frijoli Chiquita plunged a horn into one of Spradley's hind quarters, ripping it open from hock to hip. The game little horse let out a scream of pain and gave down in the rear. At this moment, and before the bull could retreat, Pickett jumped from Spradley's back and tried to fasten his arms around the enraged animal's bloodslickened horns. In three attempts, he was unable to get a secure hold. The crowd had begun to throw all sorts of objects into the ring, and Pickett, desperate and realizing that if he was to live out the day he must tie onto the brute, flung himself between the gory horns of the bull, his body directly in front, and fastened his arms around its horns. This was a very unsatisfactory position from which to bulldog (he should have been to the side and behind the horns), but at this point, Pickett was willing to try anything.

Frijoli Chiquita was surprised at this new turn of events, but only for a moment. He launched an effort to dislodge the intruder, tossing the luckless and unwelcome cowboy from side to side like a sheet in the wind. Unable to dislodge Pickett, he tried to gore him and even attempted to ram the man into the wall of the bull ring, all to no avail. Pickett stuck like a bur, despite Frijoli Chiquita's efforts and the objects thrown into the ring, and was able, to some extent, to smother the bull with his knees.

Puzzled, Frijoli Chiquita finally stopped to consider his next move. He would stand still for a few seconds, then shake Pickett vigorously, not unlike a housewife shaking a tablecloth. During this very rough treatment, a wound in Pickett's cheek (incurred while he was bulldogging a steer a few nights earlier and so large that he could have run his tongue through it), was reopened and began to bleed profusely. Then someone threw a beer bottle. It struck Pickett in the side, breaking three ribs and opening a long gash that began to stream blood down over his boots. Short of breath because of the altitude, weak, exhausted, and utterly unable to continue the struggle, Pickett let go and fell away, landing on his feet in the middle of the ring as knives, fruit, bottles, canes, cushions, cans, and rocks showered around him. He had remained on the bull's horns for seven and one-half endless, horror-filled minutes and had spent thirty-eight and one-half minutes in the ring.

Frijoli Chiquita rushed to gore the Negro cowboy, missed his arm by the breadth of a hair, then ran over Bill, knocking him down and passing over his body without inflicting serious injury. The bull squared off a second time to make the kill and was preparing to gore Pickett when a young Mexican bullfighter, a

The bit used by Pickett on his horse Spradley in his attempt to dog a Mexican fighting bull in Mexico City, December 23, 1908.

friend of Pickett, leaped into the ring and, using his vest as a cape, attracted the animal's attention, thereby giving Bill a chance to escape a bloody and horrible death. The crowd, angrier now, began to spit on the cowboys in the ring. It was necessary to run a bunch of ranch steers among the frightened horses and the bull before the horses could be coaxed out and the ring cleared.

It looked as if there would be a riot before the members of the 101 Ranch crew could leave the bull ring. They finally took refuge behind an iron gate, where they remained for nearly two hours as the mob shouted and milled in the seating section and the ring proper. Finally, President Díaz sent two hundred mounted men to escort the troupe back to the showgrounds. There were small demonstrations throughout the night, but the soldiers kept order; within twenty-four hours, all was calm again. The evening performance was presented at 8:45 without incident, as were the twice-daily shows during the next three days.

Pickett's immediate concern was not for himself but for Spradley's injuries. The horse had been able to regain his feet and had limped out of the ring. Upon examination, it was found that Spradley, lying down now, had an ugly wound, had lost a great deal of blood, and was in great pain. Pickett was grief stricken because he thought Spradley was ruined and would have to be destroyed. Just then, an ancient and wrinkled Mexican versed in the lore of the bull ring stepped forward and took charge of a lost cause. He sent a boy to fetch two ripe red — not yellow — bananas. He peeled them and thrust the ripe fruit deep into Spradley's wound, assuring everyone present that all would be well. The horse stopped quivering and groaning and lay quiet. Within ten minutes, he had regained his feet and was ready to be led away. The wound healed without swelling and left not even the hint of a limp in Spradley's gait. All that remained to remind Pickett of their terrible experience was the huge scar on Spradley's rump.

While his wounds (it took him a month to recover) were being dressed, Pickett made a statement to the press. The bull's neck was so short and thick, he said, he was unable at any time to get his hands together under it. "If I had gotten the kind of a hold I usually get and the kind I wanted," said Pickett, "I would have stayed with that bull until he starved to death, if I had been unable to throw it before."

Meanwhile, the presiding judge offered his objection to the presence of the other cowboys in the ring, and not without reason, for the announcement of the event stipulated that Pickett would go in alone. The spectators protested once more and asked that El Toro refund the money they had paid for tickets. Their request was refused. The presence of the cowboys was intended as protection for Pickett in case his life was endangered and was in no way an attempt to deceive the public, Joe and Zack Miller declared. The Millers were not acquainted with the strict regulations of the bull ring, and of course they did not consider this a deviation from the advertised program.

The public was biased from the start by the newspaper stories, the posters on the streets, the display of the wrongly worded announcement, and the unexpected action of the authorities in forcing a change of bulls at the last moment. The uncouth behavior of viewers on the sunny side of the ring was partly checked by the police; they arrested several men who were throwing oranges, cushions, and stones into the arena. Those spectators who would speak said they were aroused to envy and hatred by what they called the conceitedness of foreigners who dared to insult their national sport and that they went to the ring armed with a prejudiced mind, sticks and stones, and a resolution to take the life of a human being in order to gain satisfaction.

Let it simply be said here that there was a major breakdown in communications between the visiting Americans and the Mexican public in general. It is true that Rivero and Zack Miller both understood the terms of the contest and what was expected of Pickett to win or lose the wager, but at this point the understanding ended. It is also true that Pickett knew his job well and knew what Miller expected of him, but neither he nor Miller had the vaguest notion of what the Mexican public understood or expected of Pickett. The public knew none of this.

Thirty years earlier, there was advertised a fight between a Comanche Indian and a fighting bull, to take place at the plaza de toros on the Paseo de la Reforma. The story leads one to believe that the Indian was brutally slain by the bull and that now, in 1908, the public in general was assembled to see a repeat performance, only this time it was to be an American Negro who was to die. The Mexicans did not know the meaning of *bulldogging*. To them, an encounter between a *toro* and a *torero* had only one end result: the death of the bull or the man. Said *El Imparcial* in its editions of December 24, 1908:

Pickett defeated the bull and the crowd departed disappointed, as they were hoping to see not precisely that which they did see: they were hoping for blood and the red liquid and fumes did not darken the sand, as at other times. Pickett subdued the beast and put his snout on the ground, doubling his neck under the weight of his [Pickett's] herculean strength. But the crowd wanted blood, as that is the reason they go to the circus: blood of bulls, blood of horses, or of men; but blood which stains and darkens the grayish and monotonous sand of the bull ring. But this occasion did not give them that pleasure. Now it will be another time.

The great scandal was almost without precedent; of a type which the organizers, among whom was Don Jose del Rivero, had provided a noisy fiasco.

Even though Señor Rivero is employed at El Toro bull ring, El Toro establishment has no part in this matter. Nonetheless, we believe that a business such as El Toro ought not to have permitted its subordinate employees, as these men were, to become involved in such mockeries as that which took place yesterday. If it is so pleasing to make fun of the public, then individuals who engage in such activities become, decidedly, representatives of enterprises of that class or type.

Joe Miller collected his bet and the gate receipts, but, not content with victory, he immediately offered ten thousand pesos in gold to any matador who would duplicate Pickett's exploit. There were no takers, and Pickett informed the Millers that if there was to be any more dogging of Mexican fighting bulls, Zack himself would have to be the hero. (Incidentally, Bill Pickett's salary, as was the pay of the other 101 Ranch cowboys in Mexico, was eight dollars a week with room and board.)

Bill Pickett about 1908. This photograph was probably made in Arizona. Courtesy Johnnie Mullins.

107

There remains a question that can never be answered: Could Bill have bulldogged Frijoli Chiquita if he had been left to his own devices and if the spectators had not interfered? The merits of the struggle and its possible outcome are argued pro and con to this day. Some of the people who watched the affair say the bull was weakening at the time Pickett was forced to turn him loose and leave the ring. It was Pickett's contention until his dying day that if he had been left unmolested, he finally would have bulldogged Frijoli Chiquita. Many of the cowboys present were of the same opinion because Pickett had never before failed to dog any animal he had tied onto. The Dusky Demon even drew praise from the *Mexican Herald* which said December 24:

Foolhardy as it may have been, Pickett faced one of the most ferocious bulls, selected by the expresa after the refusal of the authorities to permit the renowned Bonito to appear, and did all in the power of a human being to accomplish a feat which has never been attempted before but which undoubtedly cannot be accomplished by any professional bullfighter in the republic even under the most favorable circumstances to say nothing of being under constant fire from an infuriated mob who were so far prejudiced as not to give the slightest recognition to the bravery of a man who has taken the almost certain chance of death never before approached by any professional bullfighter produced by either Spain or Mexico.

Pathé-Fréres was there and recorded the exciting event on film in its entirety. The footage was shown in theaters through the United States during 1909, but it has since been lost to posterity. It would be priceless today, as are the old Tom Mix films and others of that era.

Its Mexican tour over, the 101 Ranch Wild West Show packed up after the final performance on December 26 and headed north to the ranch, making stops in San Antonio and Fort Worth en route. Between San Antonio and Fort Worth, two male employees of the show blew open the safe in the ticket wagon and robbed it. Both were apprehended almost immediately, and all of the money was recovered.

The show was billed for Gainesville, Texas, but the weather was very cold and the engagement was passed up. As the train passed through Ardmore, Oklahoma, the home of Floyd Randolph, he tossed off his saddle and then jumped from the train to spend some time with his family. Before leaving, he instructed his friends to send his personal effects, which at that moment were packed in a baggage car, to him from the ranch.

The White House on the 101 Ranch as it appeared when Bill Pickett worked there. All that remains today is the foundation.

ʁ VI ʁ

THE SHOW ON THE ROAD

The show train had barely returned to Bliss from Mexico when, during the early morning hours of January 14, 1909, the palatial Miller residence, the White House, burned to the ground. Only a trunk and the baggage of some guests were saved. It is believed that the fire started in the basement, but its cause remains unknown. The ranch house was one of the finest in Oklahoma, and its contents were insured for seventy-five hundred dollars—a goodly sum in 1909.

The Millers immediately began construction of a new and bigger home on the same site. This house was to be fireproof. Steel and concrete were used, and the only portions that could burn were the floors, doors, and ornamental woodwork. The roof was constructed of asbestos material. The plans called for a seventeen-room residence containing every modern convenience and comfort, including private plants furnishing hot and cold ventilation, steam heat, hot and cold water, and electric lights. The architectural style was colonial, and massive porticos on two sides

111

gave it the appearance of an old-fashioned Southern home.

The first floor contained a large living room, den, and library and a large dining room and kitchen. The laundry was in the basement. The second floor had nine large bedrooms, each with bath, a medium-size living room or hall. The third floor was one large room; the walls were adorned with pictures of buffalo and cattle from the ranch herds. There were enough large four-poster beds to accommodate one hundred guests. The third-floor room was used during rodeo season for sleeping quarters and at other times for dances and parties to entertain visitors. A screened balcony that opened off the third floor offered a fine view of the ranch and the surrounding countryside. Throughout the home were rare rugs woven by the Indians, and on the walls were paintings by well-known artists, buffalo heads, firearms, cowboy regalia, buffalo robes, and colorful Indian blankets. The exterior, of course, was a brilliant white. The White House cost the Millers more than thirty-five thousand dollars.

The 1909 show was jointly owned by Joe, Zack, and George Miller and Edward Arlington, formerly with Pawnee Bill's wild west show. He was an extremely skilled circus man and had worked for years with the Barnum & Bailey Circus before joining Pawnee Bill.

This was the year the show was first called the Miller Brothers' 101 Ranch Real Wild West Show; however, the word *real* was not played up much in the advertisements until a few years later. The 1909 show was made up of 22 railroad cars: 9 flats, 7 horse cars, and 6 sleepers. There were 36 wagons, 16 oxen, the arena tent (which was 390 feet wide and 550 feet long), three horse tents (35 feet by 60 feet, 40 by 80, and 40 by 200), and a kitchen and dining tent (60 feet by 180 feet). The show also carried saddle horses, steers for roping and bulldogging, mules, and buffalo.

The months preceding the tour season were filled with hectic activity. There were many preparations to be made for the tour, as well as much exhausting work in taking care of 15,000 head of cattle shipped to the 101 Ranch for summer grazing. The show riders also worked on the ranch, as did the riding stock. Even the mules used to haul show baggage earned their keep on the ranch until 1910, when they were replaced by horses. The cowboys not only took care of the cattle, but their activities were used as local color and atmosphere in three films made by the Selig Polyscope Company during the early months of 1909. Featured in these western films were John Kenyon and his wife, Van E. Barrett, George L. Graves, Laura Roth, and Carroll McFarland.

Bill Pickett was still suffering from the effects of his encounter with Frijoli Chiquita and didn't remain at the ranch. Instead, he joined his family on a ranch north of Chandler, Oklahoma, where he worked in a limited capacity for his old friend Bill Shandell, a former 101 cowboy. Here he slowly recovered. Although Maggie worried about his injuries, she and their daughters were happy to have Bill home. Because he loved his work, even with its long hours and many demands, he didn't spend much time with his family. Maggie never understood why Bill couldn't be just a good working cowboy and forget the applause of the crowds. She and the girls needed him, and she and Bill exchanged many harsh words about his being away from home so much.

The Pickett girls loved their father and always enjoyed the stories he told them about his life on tour: the excitement of the crowds, the strange cities, the colorful. parades, the dangers of bulldogging and bronc riding. The names of well-known trick riders and other performers with fancy acts were familiar to the girls and their mother. Yet there was always a thread of sadness in Bill's voice as he told them about his work. He could never forget his two sons who died in infancy. Were they alive, he could train them to follow in his footsteps. Maggie was well aware of Bill's sorrow and kept silent.

The 1909 show program began with a grand entry that featured a stagecoach, an overland freight wagon, and Indian women using travois. These three modes of transportation were familiar to residents of the West but were not so well known to folks in other parts of the country. Behind the travois came the many displays that made up the show. In the second, which consisted of seventeen introductions, each group or individual rushed into the arena, dust flying as they took their places before the audience. Colorfully dressed Indians and Cossacks, *vaqueros* and *rurales*, cowboys and cowgirls filled the arena. After them came the individual performers; Prince Lucca, chief of the Cossacks; Chief Eagle Feather; Vern Tantlinger; and Zack Miller, bronzed by the Oklahoma sun, sturdy and steel eyed, waving his big white Stetson and wearing chaps, tooled cowboy boots, and a

Bill Pickett with Joe Miller near the 101 Ranch Wild West Show's Indian village. Miller is mounted on his horse Chester.

silk shirt. A colorful kerchief was knotted around his neck.

Display Three was a re-creation of the Pony Express in all its trials and dangers as it carried the mail on the western frontier during 1860 and 1861.

The star performers, all expert ropers, demonstrated their skill in the fourth display. Some of them later held world titles. In this group were Chester Byers, Sam Garrett, Mabel Miller, Esteven Clemento, Otto Kline, Guy Weadick and his wife Florence LaDue, Johnny Frantz, Vern and Edith Tantlinger, Pat Christman, John Mullens, and Frank Maish (he joined the show during the tour). Some of the ropers also had other skills and in some instances became better known for these. Not all of the performers remained with the show throughout the season; instead, they alternated between it and the 101 Ranch, being assigned wherever they were needed.

One of the most exciting acts came in Display Five. It featured the colorful and expert driving of Hank Walker, known as Rocky Mountain. He drove the overland stage at top speed around the arena as no other man could. Close on his heels was a band of outlaws who always overtook the stage, robbed its screaming passengers, and, amid protests, blew open the strongbox. However, before the bandits could escape, the cowboys from the ranch got the valuables back to the passengers and the gold returned to the strongbox. Then, firing pistols and rifles, they pursued the outlaws out of the arena. One of the horses, called Eagle, was hit, fell wounded, then got up and limped from the field. This portion of the display never failed to draw rapt attention from the spectators.

Nothing was more colorful than the Indians performing their many dances in front of the grandstand during the sixth display. The beat of their drums and the grace of their steps always drew applause.

Cowboys riding the fleetest horses from the 101 Ranch corrals filled the arena in Display Seven. Their performance consisted of snatching objects from the ground while riding at breakneck speed.

Amelia Summerville and her horse Columbus sparkled in Display Eight. Preceding her were the 101

Ranch High School Horses, a group highly trained to perform tricks. Zack Miller worked with Amelia and later in the 1909 season trained his Arabian stallion Ben Hur to perform the same tricks. She and Columbus left the 101 show after the last performance at New Haven, Connecticut, and joined California Frank's Wild West Show. Maude Burbank and her horse Dynamo replaced Amelia and Columbus at Meriden, Connecticut.

The ninth display was Roman riding. Part of it was done by John Ray and W. Weideman, Roman standing riders. As they performed, Melvin Saunders vaulted over four horses and landed on a fifth. All this was accompanied by military music.

Next came the biggest act, the one with which the Miller brothers had gained renown in show business: bulldogging. During 1909 and succeeding years, the Millers capitalized on Bill Pickett's adventure in Mexico and made him a headliner in all the show's publicity, building the program around his performance. Since Pickett was still too stove up to accompany the show, Dell Blancett dogged for him until August, when he got married and left the show to compete at Cheyenne's Frontier Days. Vester Pegg, John Ray, and Esteven Clemento took turns for a while when Blancett was laid up with an injury sustained at Bridgeport, Connecticut, as he was bulldogging a steer. After Blancett left, Clemento did most of the dogging until he was badly gored at Kalamazoo, Michigan. Thereafter, Ray and Pegg filled in for him. Early in September, Pickett bade his family farewell and joined the show for the rest of the season.

After Pickett's performance, a herd of bawling Longhorns raced into the arena. They were followed by two cowboys, a header and a heeler, who demonstrated steer roping and riding. They cut one steer out of the herd and roped it. After the animal regained its feet, a rider mounted it and it was turned loose to buck its way back to the herd. Cowgirls as well as cowboys did the riding.

Display Twelve was quite different. Vern Tantlinger, who for many seasons was recognized as chief of the cowboys with the 101 Ranch show, demonstrated his skill with the boomerang. He and his wife, Edith, were known as fancy ropers, but his specialty was the boomerang. He was assisted by Zu-Rah, billed as an Australian aborigine, who caught the returning boomerang.

One of the most beautiful displays was the Quadrille on Horseback. Participating in it were Bertha Ross, Florence LaDue, Maude Jameson, Edyth Christman, Dolly Mullens, Mary Fitzpatrick, Marie Morrison, and Marie Killinger. Each had a cowboy partner.

Display Fourteen featured beautiful Chan-Tu-Ka-Wea, an Oklahoma Indian girl, and Edith Tantlinger. Their specialty was fancy trap shots.

That which happened often in real life on the western plains was enacted in Display Fifteen. A cowboy's horse was stolen, he pursued the thief, and amid much action, the thief was caught.

Display Sixteen was Prince Lucca and his Cossacks, bedecked in all their finery. They were hard, rough riders, and theirs was a contest to prove that in horsemenship the cowboys would come out second best;

Bill Pickett on his dogging horse Croppie with the show tent
in the background.

the spectators were left to decide which group was better. This was a dangerous act. One of the Cossacks was nearly dragged to death after his horse stumbled in a performance at Davenport, Iowa, and Prince Lucca fractured his shoulder on the slippery ground when the show played in Fort Worth, Texas.

Trick and fancy riders were the stars in Display Seventeen. They included Vester Pegg, who leaped from the back of a running horse to that of another which was neither saddled nor bridled. Others working in this display were Otto Kreinbeck, George Hooker, W. Weideman, Bill Selman, and Dan Dix.

Shooting airborne objects from the back of a running horse was the thrill of Display Eighteen. Vern Tantlinger and Princess Weona were the stars.

Display Nineteen always brought spectators to their feet as they yelled and cheered the men and women riding outlaw horses in the bucking contest. In full view of the audience, the animal was snubbed down, blindfolded, and saddled. Amid kicks and jumps, the rider mounted, the blind was pulled off, and the bronc took off. Some of the well-known riders participating in this event were Bill Pickett, Vester Pegg, George Hooker, Johnnie Frantz, Goldie St. Clair, Bertha Ross, and Marie Killinger.

The twentieth and final display was a re-creation of one of the saddest chapters in Oklahoma history: the massacre of Pat Hennessey and his party. Cheyenne Indians attacked the group July 4, 1875, on the Chisholm Trail near the present site of Hennessey, Oklahoma. Hennessey, a freighter, used the trail often, but on that fateful day, he and everyone with him were killed. Hennessey was lashed to a wagon wheel and the wagon was set afire. When U.S. Marshal W. H. Malaley arrived, this was what he saw. To add realism to the 101 Ranch Wild West Show version, Malaley was on hand to do exactly what he did at the massacre. Chief Bull Bear, who led the attack, also was in the arena.

The 1909 show opened at Ponca City on April 14, with commitments in Oklahoma until May 2. It appeared in Kansas City, Missouri, on May 3 and 4. The next stop was Indianopolis, followed by a two-day stand at Cincinnati beginning on May 10. Most of the May performances were in Ohio and Pennsylvania; June and July were spent in New England. By late September, the show had worked its way west to Wichita Falls, Texas, after which the equipment was shipped to East St. Louis, Illinois, for the winter. The cowboys and livestock returned to the home ranch.

Business was good at nearly all of the stops, and especially encouraging from a financial standpoint were the performances in New England. There were many mishaps along the road: four wagons were demolished in a train accident at Columbus, Ohio, and several mules were badly injured at Wichita Falls when one of the stock cars was wrecked. Injuries to key performers continued to be a problem. Serious human accidents were mostly confined to the bulldoggers and bronc busters and steer riders, which pointed up the hazards in these three divisions of the show. Pickett was fortunate during the month he was with the show and didn't incur additional injuries.

Joe Haskell, son of Oklahoma's first governor, Charles N. Haskell, visited the show during the 1909 season. He was well acquainted with the Millers and

Six of the cowgirls on the 101 Ranch during Bill Pickett's time. Note the ranch buildings in the background.

was invited to appear with the show as a cowboy, which he did, during the stand in Boston.

In November, several key members of the 101 Ranch show joined the IXL Ranch Wild West Show for a winter tour of South America. The first performance was in Buenos Aires, Argentina, on December 18. Among those making the tour were George Hooker, Chester Byers, Vester Pegg, Frank Maish,

Ethel and Juanita Perry, Jim Garrett, Johnnie Frantz, and Vern and Edith Tantlinger. The show docked in New York on April 4, 1910, and the 101 Ranch personnel left at once for St. Louis, where their show was scheduled to make its first stand of the new season from April 16 through Aprill 22.

In January 1910, Bill Pickett moved his family into a large, comfortable house east of Bliss on a leased section of the 101 Ranch several miles from ranch headquarters. Several of the Pickett children have said their father owned this property, but land records fail to verify their claim. The new home was much closer to Pickett's work than Ponca City, and he was able to spend more time with his family.

During the 1910 season's parades, Pickett rode atop one of the wagons with two buffalo, Nip and Mary. (Nip is reputed to be the one whose likeness is on the old U.S. nickel.) Bill and a cowboy called Frenchy handled the buffalo with the show; Bill was in charge of the herd, always numbering fifty or more, at the ranch. They were used for show and breeding stock, the Millers selling many animals to other ranchers.

The usual number of casualties among bronc and steer riders and bulldoggers occurred during the season, but none was very serious. Bill Pickett was the star attraction, of course. He had fully recovered from his bout with Frijoli Chiquita, and his performance improved each year. He never failed to respond to the challenge of each new steer, and the applause from the crowd never failed to encourage him to take more risks in an effort to satisfy his tremendous desire to remain the world's first and greatest bulldogger. He rode broncs and steers, but dogging remained his special realm of proficiency.

The 1910 season closed at West Point, Mississippi, on November 19. Eastern winter quarters were established at Passaic, New Jersey. The show's equipment was sent there, but the stock was shipped to the ranch.

The 1911 season opened on April 9 with a week-long stand at the Boston Arena. After leaving Massachusetts, the show toured Pennsylvania, Michigan, Illinois, Wisconsin, Oklahoma, Texas, and California. The program remained almost unchanged, but in the show's huge newspaper advertisements, Pickett was the only performer listed by name:

Pickett Dusky Demon of Oklahoma reproducing his Fight for Life in a Mexican Bull Ring. Only man in human history who ever battled barehanded with a Spanish bull and escaped alive. To be seen in a life-risking exploit at every 101 Ranch Wild West performance, and nowhere else.

This ad was perhaps a little misleading to the average reader in that it may have implied something different from Pickett's regular performance. In fact, Bill's act was his well-perfected bulldogging, as it always had been. It might be well to remember that this was what he was attempting to do in the bull ring at Mexico City.

An advertisement for the 101 Ranch Wild West Show headlining Bill Pickett.

Only Wild West Show Coming!

The Largest of Its Kind in Existence. *1913*

Labor Day's Sole Attraction.   Camp Ground—Race Track

DECATUR MONDAY SEPT. 1

MILLER BROS. & EDW. ARLINGTON'S

101 RANCH REAL WILD WEST

THE WEST AS IT WAS

Excelled by GREATER AMERICA'S GREAT OUTDOOR SHOW which has advanced in three years to the heights of successfulness. The sensation and furore of New York City and every other big city of the Republic. The triumphal invader of Mexico and the conquering visitor to Canada

WILD GLORIES OF THE VANISHED BORDER

Annual holiday tour of the Cowboys, Cowgirls and Indians of the most famous Ranch in the world. True and typical of range and roundup. The only exposition of Frontier Life and history in its original kind and scope. Without a counterpart on earth and by very nature and scenes impossible of imitation or duplication.

Largest Exclusive Western Show in Existence

PICKETT, Dusky Demon of Oklahoma

Only man in Human History who ever fought, barehanded, a Spanish Bull. Positive feature of every exhibition

More performers, more cars, more seats, bigger tents than any and all other amusement undertakings, depicting solely frontier scenes and incidents. Cowboys, Wild West Girls, Indians, Mexicans, Rurales, Vacqueros, Senoritas, Scouts, Pioneers, Homesteaders, Pony Express Celebrities, Champions of the Gun and Lariat, Bucking Horses, Buffaloes, Long-horned Steers united in an enlightening, spectacular tournament, differing radically and fundamentally from all familiar others. As big and perfect a show as humanly possible

2 P.M.—TWO PERFORMANCES RAIN OR SHINE 8 P.M.

POSITIVE FORENOON STREET PARADE

Traversing the principal thoroughfares and displaying the unexampled magnitude and mesh of the great enterprise

See the Auto Polo

First Time Here

THE THRILLER OF THE CENTURY

The Acme of Sensationalism.

Iron Tail—The Indian Chief whose head appears on the new 5 cent piece.

Reserved Seat Sale Exhibition Day at West's Drug Store at same prices as those prevailing at grounds.

Billboard magazine's issue of August 15, 1911, called Bill Pickett "the modern Urus, in a demon-stration of courage, nerve, strength and agility in which he duplicates his feat of conquering a Spanish fighting bull, unarmed and unaided, by forcing the largest of bulls to the tanbark by sheer strength."

The season closed in the Los Angeles area late in November. Venice, California, was selected for winter quarters because it was near a film studio. A contract had been signed with the Bison Moving Picture Com-pany, and production, using show personnel and property, began that winter. At least two films pro-duced by the Thomas H. Ince Studio at Inceville on the Malibu Coast also involved 101 Ranch property and performers.

Bill Pickett and most of the show personnel shipped back to the ranch, where they worked at various jobs and made preparations for the 1912 season. Bill's sal-ary had not been raised, by any means, in proportion to his popularity in the arena. He was still getting twelve dollars a week and keep. However, he and his family were furnished a home near Bliss; they had a cow and a few hogs and raised a garden.

The 1912 season opened in Santa Monica on March 23. The program remained unchanged, but there was one unusual thing about it: the show did not appear east of Ohio. It toured California, Nevada, Utah, Montana, Washington, and British Columbia, then went back to Washington and Oregon, returned to British Columbia, traveled to the Dakotas, Minnesota, Iowa, Wisconsin, Illinois, and Ohio, and finally doubled back to Iowa, Texas, Arkansas, and Louisiana. Milt Hinkle was with the W. A. Dickey Wild West Show at Montreal on July 4. He says Bill Pickett also was with the show and that some of the steers they bulldogged weighed eleven hundred pounds. The 101 Ranch show was in the area at the time, and Pickett held his usual prominent place on the program. The season ended in Hot Springs, Arkansas, on November 16. The show property was winter-quartered there, but, again as usual, the stock and most of the hands returned to the ranch.

Two accidents involving animals and equipment occurred during the season. On the run to Milwaukee, a fire broke out in the wagons in which the horse tents were stored, but it was discovered and extinguished before it had caused much damage. A more serious mishap occurred between Plattville and Lancaster, Wisconsin. Four cars were wrecked, five head of baggage stock and five arena horses were killed, twenty-five other horses were injured, and the calliope was destroyed. Additional horses were secured in Chicago, and an old calliope was purchased.

During the winter of 1912-13, Bill Pickett spent his time breaking horses and steers for the 1913 season, which opened at Hot Springs, Arkansas, on April 5 and used approximately the same route followed in 1911. Pickett spent the season with the show as its chief attraction and bulldogger, still the only performer named on the program. Among the ropers, riders, and bulldoggers were Chester Byers, Montana Jack Ray, Tommy Kirnan, Hank Durnell, Grover and Clarence Schultz, Ed and Eadie Lindsey, Bee-Ho Gray and his wife, Lafe Lewman, Milt Hinkle, Ida Somerville, Tom Eckhardt, Billy and Tony Binder, Pascale Perry, Harry Smith, Buck Stewart, Weaver and Juanita Gray, Ethel and Juanita Perry, Mabel Kline, Beatrice Brosseau, Lulu Parr, Jane Fuller, Blanch McGaughey, O'Dell Osborn, Martha Allen, and Vera McGuiness. The show closed on Tuesday, October 28 at Houston, Texas.

Winter quarters for stock and cowboys were the home ranch, but most of the equipment was shipped to Lakeview, New Jersey, where it was repaired and stored to await an eastern opening in 1914. During the 1913 season, the show traveled in twenty-eight wooden railroad cars: six sleepers, eight stock cars (twenty-eight head to a car), and fourteen flats.

⧏ **VII** ⧐

SOUTH AMERICAN
AND BRITISH TOURS

Near the end of the 1913 season, Edward Arlington, a partner in the 101 Ranch Wild West Show and owner of the rolling stock, began to put together a show he planned to send to South America during the winter of 1913-14. On the proposed route from New York were Buenos Aires, Montevedeo, Rio de Janeiro, and points between. Among the performers, hired from the 101 Ranch show and Buffalo Bill's wild west show, were Bill Pickett, World Champion Trick Roper Chester Byers, Hank Durnell, Harry Smith, Otto Kline, Milt Hinkle, Charlie Aldridge, Bob Anderson, Billy Lorette, Lulu Parr, Mabel Kline, Beau Brosseau, Jane Fuller, and Iona Hinkle.

After the final performance of the 101 Ranch Wild West Show at Houston three baggage cars were loaded with gear, horses and saddles and shipped to New York for the South American tour.

The cowboys, cowgirls, and Indians who signed on the tour went to New York by train and were met by Edward Arlington. The show left Brooklyn from Pier 9 on November 1, 1913, aboard the *Varsara*. Arlington and Roy Chandler bossed the show, and Vern Tantlinger was the arena director. The voyage south was rough and stormy, and most of the people were seasick. Hank Durnell came down with smallpox and begged to be thrown overboard because he was so sick; he later recovered. Four of the Indians died of smallpox. The ship's crew sewed them in canvas and buried them at sea.

Bill Pickett became so seasick that he wondered whether he would ever see Maggie and his girls again. He had never been on an ocean before, never so sick, never so far away from the solid ground of the plains. He said he never expected to arrive in Buenos Aires alive, but he did, with the show, after a voyage of twenty-five days. Arlington did a fine job of bribing the health inspector, and the ship was not quarantined. The show wasn't out of trouble, however, because the livestock inspector discovered that one of the horses had glanders, a highly infectious disease. He ordered all of the horses killed and burned. Although Pickett had been a little reluctant to ship Spradley back to the 101 Ranch, he was now elated that his favorite horse was not among those being destroyed.

The show was set up at the Park of the Japanese. Arlington selected Milt Hinkle, Charlie Aldridge, and Harry Smith to go on a stock-buying trip. They bought twenty-five saddle horses, seven steers—three for bulldogging and four to ride—and a mule for Billy Lorette's clown act. The newspapers gave the show good publicity, and people turned out in throngs to see it. In fact, on some days, three performances were uncorked to accommodate the large crowds. Bill

Pickett's bulldogging was especially well received. After winding up its tour in Rio de Janeiro, the troupe shipped for home in time to open the 1914 season at New York's Madison Square Garden on April 20.

Before the 1914 season opened, the British government invited the Miller brothers to bring their show to London to celebrate the Century of Peace (between the English-speaking nations); the show was to be part of the Anglo-American Exposition. The proposition looked like a money-maker, and the Millers and Arlington decided to accept it.

Buck Jones (Charles Gibhart) joined the show as a bronc rider and trick roper. It was here that he met his future wife, Julia Allen, an equestrienne. Jones became one of Hollywood's most widely known western movie stars, playing his first leading role in *The Last Straw* in 1919. By 1924, starring in *The Rough Riders*, he was one of the biggest box-office attractions Fox Studios had. His last picture was *Dawn on the Great Divide*, filmed in 1942. During a career that spanned twenty-three years, he averaged eight pictures a year and was never linked to a scandal of any kind. His career was cut short while he was on a War Bond tour: he died in the Coconut Grove fire at Boston in November 1942.

Pickett appeared on the 101 Ranch Wild West Show program in Madison Square Garden as a headliner and bulldogged steers for the full engagement. His act was as smooth as silk, except for one show. When playing the Garden, it was customary to place a cowboy at ringside near each entrance during the riskier acts as a safeguard for the audience in case a wild steer broke loose. The practice was especially enforced while the bulldogging was in progress. On this particular evening, Billy Binder, (he had a small wild west show before 1914, when he went to work for the 101) was guarding one of the entrances. Bill waited for the chute man to turn his steer into the arena. The steer was wild and big (since this was the first stand of a new season, the stock was all very green) and came out of the chute under a full head of steam, heading with all haste for Oklahoma and home. He crossed the foul line; Pickett took after him at a full gallop but was unable to close the gap. The steer reached the opposite side of the arena and the aisle guarded by Binder and, without a moment's hesitation, headed up the ramp into the seats. Binder tied on to the animal as it passed him, but with little success: he was dragged up a flight of stairs. Pickett rode his horse up the stairs and grappled with the steer, and he and Binder finally were able to get the critter back down into the ring again. Bill tried a second steer and dogged him without incident.

After the New York engagement, the Millers and Arlington split the show and sent one section to England. For the most part, it was made up of the people who took the South American trip, including Bill Pickett, Guy Weadick and Florence LaDue, Milt Hinkle, Zack Miller, Sam Garrett, George Hooker, Johnny Baker, Chester Byers, Fred and Ed Burns, Stack Lee, Hank Durnell, Lottie Shaw, Lucille Mann, Alice Lee, Mabel Clive, Lottie Aldridge, Babe Willetts, Dot Vernon, Ruth Roach, and Jane Fuller. Bill Pickett's act was the star attraction.

The show opened in late May at the Anglo-American Exposition in remodeled Shepherd's Bush Stadium in London. There were two ninety-minute shows daily, at 3:30 and 8:30 P.M. The show played to record crowds and many distinguished guests, including King George V and Queen Mary of England, Empress Alexandra and Dowager Empress Marie of Russia, Sir Thomas Lipton and scores of the nobility.

The humane societies took exception to Pickett's bulldogging and had him arrested for being cruel to animals. The newspapers gave the incident widespread coverage. Pickett was fined twenty-five dollars, but this did not stop the act; Zack Miller felt it was cheap advertising and made a deal whereby Pickett was fined each week. Said one Briton: "British have peculiar views on the handling of animals. You could beat a child and only be fined, but do the same to a dog and there would be a public outcry."

Pickett's bulldogging was as popular in England as it had been at home and brought him much acclaim. He was invited by the Earl of Lonsdale to dine at the earl's castle and meet his children, who wanted to see a black man who could throw a steer with his teeth. Bill accepted the invitation but was confused about how to use the flatware and got little to eat (in fact, he had to make out his meal on leftovers in the cook tent when he got back to the show).

One of the highlights of the British tour was the bulldogging of a wild Scottish Highland steer selected as a worthy challenger to Pickett's skill. The Dusky Demon dogged the animal without difficulty and received a roar of approval from a full house. One day, he was approached by an Englishman who offered to bet that he could not bulldog his steer that night. Bill replied that he had dogged his steer the day before.

133

Said the Englishman: "You might have accomplished the feat yesterday, but you can't do it again today." Bill covered the bet and won it easily.

Rider and roper George Hooker was reported to have made a big splash with some of the ladies and was very much in demand as an escort. Hooker, who hailed from Arizona, was a large man of Negro and Mexican extraction and a good showman.

War clouds in Europe were becoming ever darker, and it seemed certain that hostilities soon would break out between England and Germany. The show went great guns for six months, and Zack Miller was thinking of touring the Continent when a royal courier delivered the following message:

National Emergency   Impressment Order Under Section
115 of the Army Act
To Zack T. Miller, 68 Holland Rd. W.

His Majesty, having declared that a national emergency has arisen, the horses and vehicles of the 101 Ranch Show are to be impressed for public service if found fit (in accordance with Section 115 of the Army Act), and will be paid for on the spot at the market value to be settled by the purchasing officer. Should you not accept the price paid as fair value, you have the right to appeal to the County Court (in Scotland the Sheriff's Court), but you must not hinder the delivery of the horses and vehicles, etc. The purchasing officer may claim to purchase such harness and stable gear as he may require with the horse or vehicle.

Charles Carpenter, Sergt.
Place Shepherd's Bush Exhibition
Date 7th August, 1914

After the 101 show property had been rustled by the British government for its war effort against Kaiser Wilhelm's Germany, there remained only a handful of horses, a wagon or so, some miscellaneous equipment, a harness, and the show personnel. Zack Miller received some seventeen thousand pounds (approximately eighty thousand dollars) in British banknotes, but the 101 Ranch Real Wild West Show was ruined.

It was difficult to book passage home. No one wanted to sail on British ships for fear of being torpedoed by the Germans. Most of the show personnel shipped out on the American mail ship *St. Paul*, but it was several weeks before all were able to secure passage home.

The Ponca Indians and their chief, White Eagle, had been friends of the Miller family since the Indians first settled in the Cherokee Strip. They had been uprooted from their home in the Dakotas and were awaiting arrangements by the federal government and the Cherokees to settle in the Cherokee Nation. The chief and his people were heartsick and weary when George W. Miller and his son Joe first met them. G. W. knew the land of the Cherokees and felt the Poncas eventually would be happy there, so he told them of the lush grass in the valleys, the wild turkeys and prairie chickens, and the clear streams of water for their ponies. From that time on, the Poncas and the Millers were the best of friends.

The Millers rented thousands of acres from the Poncas, by whom G. W. was affectionately called Tescanudahunga (Biggest Cow Boss). To an Indian, friendship worked both ways and was more highly regarded than money. When a member of Chief White Eagle's tribe was hungry, he went to the Millers. When broke, he went to the 101 Ranch. When he needed advice about the white man's strange ways and laws, he headed for his friends at the White House.

White Eagle tolerated white man's religion but clung steadfastly to his own. Joe Miller was made a member of the tribe and sat in its councils to give advice. White Eagle almost converted Joe to his belief about the hereafter during their years of friendship. It was therefore a particularly hard blow to Joe when White Eagle, principal chief of the Poncas for more than fifty years, died in February 1914 at the age of seventy-four. He was buried in the Indian cemetery at White Eagle, Oklahoma. The chief was carefully dressed in the finest clothing of his office, and his favorite horse was killed according to ancient tribal custom for use on the way to the Happy Hunting Ground. His face was painted with clay pigment in the prescribed ritual; his feathered war bonnet and a necklace made of caputred scalps were buried with him. The grave was covered with food to sustain him until he reached the Land of the Great Spirit, and a large American flag was placed on a tall pole, as is the custom of the Poncas, and left there to the wind and rain. At the funeral were many of his friends, both red, white, and black.

An incident worthy of mention occurred during the stay in winter quarters. It involved Billy Binder, Sr., and the slaughterhouse on the ranch. Zack Miller had bought, in Fort Worth, 225 head of Mexican bulls just out of quarantine and had shipped them to the ranch, where they were to be butchered to fill contracts for beef at the Indian agencies. Now these bulls were very wild and full of fight, just off the Mexican range and not accustomed to being near human beings. The regular butcher was ill, and Binder, who as a boy had been apprenticed to a butcher, was pressed into service by the Millers.

Bill Pickett, Billy Binder, and Mexican Joe (Jose Barrera, who was later with Pawnee Bill and his show) drove several of the bulls into the catch pen adjoining the slaughterhouse. Bill and Joe went on to attend to other ranch chores, leaving Billy to tend to the day's butchering. Binder dressed out the first two bulls without incident.

The procedure was to lasso an animal with a rope that ran through a ring in the middle of the twenty-foot-square kill and dressing floor and on to a windlass in one corner, then pull it into position for killing. Billy roped his third bull without difficulty and began to wind him in. However, this bull was large, ferocious, and had his own ideas about the rough treatment he was receiving. He lunged against the rope with all his strength; it parted with a loud crack. The bull then began to make a shambles of the place. Binder was barely able to jump into the corner behind the post on which the windlass was mounted as the animal charged him. The closest help was at the ranch commissary a quarter-mile away. While dodging the bull in his meager shelter behind the windlass, Billy began to yell for help.

Bill Pickett happened to be riding by and heard cries for help coming from the slaughterhouse. He rode over and looked through the window. Binder told him to go quickly to the commissary, get a rifle from Whitie Biggers, the manager, and kill the bull.

Bill got the rifle, rode Spradley up to one of the windows and knocked out a pane of glass, shot the bull, and saved his good friend Binder from a horrible death.

During the winter of 1914-15, a seven-reel old-time Bison movie was filmed at the ranch. Pickett and other cowboys worked on and in it.

The show was again on the road in 1915. During the season, a new headliner was added in the person of Jess Willard, world champion heavyweight boxer, who proved to be a great attraction. He became champ on April 5, 1915, by knocking out Jack Johnson in the twenty-sixth round at Havana, Cuba. This was just before Willard joined the 101 show for the 1915 season. He had received good newspaper publicity for his fight, and since everyone was anxious to see the new champion in person, he was a first-rate drawing card. Willard was featured in the parade and in the sideshow, where he sparred with various challengers in demonstrating his ability and the way in which he knocked out Johnson for the championship. Pickett remained a star attraction with his bulldogging throughout the year and also rode broncs.

For several months during the 1915 season, one section of the 101 Ranch show performed just outside the grounds of the Panama-Pacific International Exposition in San Francisco. Butch Cassidy (Robert Leroy Parker), leader of the Wild Bunch, supposedly killed in Bolivia by the army in 1911, was reported by cowboy Joe Marsters to have attended one of the performances. Marsters, a bronc rider with the show, claimed he had ridden with the Wild Bunch at the age of fourteen. He told Bill Pickett Cassidy was at the show, but since Bill wasn't acquainted with Cassidy, he was unable to identify him.

The 101 Ranch show reached its largest size during the seasons from 1913 through 1915. The show train was made up of two sections, the first containing fifteen cars (four sleepers, six flats, five horse cars) and twenty wagons, the second seventeen cars (four sleepers, seven flats, and six horse cars) and forty-one wagons, a carriage and two automobiles. At the close of the 1915 season, the equipment and stock were shipped to the ranch at Bliss, where they were quartered for the winter.

William F. ("Buffalo Bill") Cody was a new headliner with the show for the 1916 season. The frontiersman served with the U.S. Army as a scout in the Indian Wars and as a showman was largely responsible for romanticizing the Cowboy West. Cody was a Pony Express Rider, served in the Civil War with the Seventh Kansas Cavalry, and in 1867-68 hunted buffalo for the Kansas Pacific Railroad to feed its workmen (hence the nickname). He served as chief of scouts under General Philip H. Sheridan four years with the Fifth U.S. Cavalry. Cody organized his own wild west show, an outdoor exhibition that dramatized contemporary western scene. It remained on the road thirty years.

The 1916 season was much like the previous three except for the Chicago program, which was a rodeo-type show. The Millers could read the handwriting on the wall: the war in Europe was getting hotter, and the United States was sure to become involved.

They also felt that transportation for the show would become more and more of a problem and that there was money to be made at the ranch under a wartime economy. At the close of the season, they decided to sell their interests to Edward Arlington with the understanding that he would not use *Miller Brothers* or *101* in connection with the show. Jess Willard was reported to have put up part of the purchase price of the action. The 101 Ranch records show a net profit of $800,000 for the period 1908-1916.

ᴿ VIII ᴿ

A NEW ERA IN RODEOS
AND WILD WEST SHOWS

Early in August 1916, the New York Stampede was
held at Sheepshead Bay Speedway in Brooklyn under
the direction of promoter and producer Guy Weadick,
who advertised it throughout the nation. It was to
run 12 days longer than rodeos being held in the
West at this time, and the prize money was more than
had ever been offered in a rodeo or cowboy contest
anywhere in the world.

The New York Stampede was on the lips of every
cowboy in the country, and many made the trip to
compete. Among the contestants and categories were
these: Mike Hastings, Ed Lindsey; *Saddle Bronc Riding,* Emery LaGrande, Rufus Rollen, Lee Caldwell,
Hoot Gibson; *Bareback Bronc Riding,* Jack Fretz,
Claude Ames, Leonard Stroud, Jesse Stahl (the outstanding black cowboy from California); *Cowboy Trick
and Fancy Roping,* Chester Byers, Bee-Ho Gray, Tex
McLeod, Sam Garrett, Johnny Judd; *Cowboy Relay
Racing,* Bob Lieche, Dwight Zediker, Roy Kivett,
Charlie Aldridge, Harry Walters; *Cowboy Trick Rid-*

ing, Leonard Stroud, Tommy Kirnan, Floyd Irwin, Harry Walters, Frank Maish; *Cowboy Steer Roping,* Henry Grammer, Fred Beeson, Johnny Murray, Clay McGonigal, Bert Weir, Charley Weir; *Cowgirl Relay Racing,* Helen Maish, Frances Irwin, Fanny Sperry Steele, Edith Irwin, Ollie Osborn; *Cowgirl Bronc Riding, Slick,* Tillie Baldwin; *Cowgirl Trick Riding,* Tillie Baldwin, Bea Kirnan, Lottie Vandreau, Peggy Warren; *Cowgirl Trick Roping,* Florence LaDue, Lucille Mulhall, Emily McLeod, Frances Irwin; *Cowgirl Bronc Riding, Hobbled,* Prairie Lillie Allen, Louise Thompson, Fox Hastings. They came from the American West—Oklahoma, California, Wyoming, Texas, New Mexico, Minnesota, Montana, Oregon, Kansas, Nebraska, Colorado—and from Canada.

Bill Pickett, referred to by the *New York Times* as "The Famous Cowboy Bill Pickett," bulldogged his first steer in twenty-six seconds. However, an argument broke out between Charles B. Irwin and Ed Lindsey over whether Pickett had hoolihaned his steer. (Hoolihaning is the fine art of alighting on the neck and horns of a steer with such force and skill as to knock him to the ground without twisting him down. The practice is barred in bulldogging contests.) The argument grew into a fight, but it was soon broken up and the dogging continued. The first day's crowd was fifteen thousand, but by the end of the stampede, it had swelled to twenty-five thousand per day. Theodore Roosevelt visited the rodeo, and Will Rogers was on hand nearly every day.

Will Rogers invited his old friends among the cowgirls and cowboys to the Ziegfeld Follies on the roof of the New Amsterdam Theatre on the last night of the stampede. Will was appearing as a headliner with his fancy roping, dancing, and witty comments on the news and various persons. That evening, he introduced various cowboys and cowgirls during his act and had them perform for the audience. It is reasonable to assume that Bill Pickett was present because he was a good friend of Will and was much admired by the humorist. In fact, Will had eaten many meals with Bill and Maggie Pickett in their home. Both Rogers and Pickett were part Cherokee, as was Tom Mix's wife Olive and daughter Ruth. Rogers, whose shrewd, homey comments about men and women and world affairs gave him widespread popularity on stage, in radio and motion pictures, and as a writer for national newspapers, was killed in an airplane crash in Alaska in 1935.

Tom Mix told this story about Will: "There was a three-foot elm stump on the Mulhall ranch near the bunkhouse that Will practiced trick roping on, and by the time he had learned how, the stump was worn down even with the ground." Will was appearing in vaudeville in 1905 after appearing with the Cummings and Mulhall Wild West Show at the St. Louis World's Fair (Louisiana Purchase Exposition) in 1904. He performed rope tricks, receiving fifteen dollars a week for his services. Pickett and Rogers appeared in the show together for several weeks.

On the final day of the New York Stampede, Emery LaGrande was declared World Champion Bronc Rider and was awarded the fifteen hundred dollar prize money. Ed Lindsey received one thousand dollars as

World Champion Bulldogger. He won a total of four thousand seven hundred dollars in the various events he entered. The best single day's time in bulldogging went to Mike Hastings for his twelve seconds flat. Henry Grammer was declared World Champion Steer Roper, and Chester Byers won the World Champion Fancy Roping title. During these years, each rodeo or cowboy contest declared its own world champion in each event, and the winner of the bronc riding contest was declared the World Champion Cowboy. It was possible to win any one of these titles several times in the course of a year, and this was accomplished regularly by many cowboys.

Today, champions in each rodeo event are selected by a system in which points are totaled at the end of the rodeo season, and the winner is the cowboy or cowgirl who has accumulated the most points during the season. The World Champion Cowboy is the man who has amassed the most points during the season, and he must have competed in several different events. The Rodeo Cowboys Association supervises the procedure and selects the winners each year.

The New York Stampede was a financial failure, but it was a milestone in rodeo history. For the most part, the people in the East had never heard of a rodeo and had very little understanding of just what transpired. The stampede changed this. Those who saw the stampede loved it, and the press gave it good coverage. Easterners then began to hear of such great rodeos as Oklahoma's Dewey Roundup, Oregon's Pendleton Round-Up, Wyoming's Cheyenne Frontier Days, Arizona's Prescott Frontier Days, and Canada's

Calgary Stampede. New York and Madison Square Garden eventually became home to world-champion rodeo for many years.

The New York rodeo over, many cowboys and cowgirls headed for Chicago and a nine-day roundup, under the supervision of Buffalo Bill Cody, to be held from August 19 through August 27 at the old Cubs baseball park at Polk Street and Lincoln Avenue. The event was promoted by the 101 Ranch show, and most of the contestants were members of the show. The *Chicago Herald* reported there were more than 300 entrants in the various contests, and the *Chicago Daily News* noted that fifty thousand dollars in prize money had been put up. One thousand dollars was being offered to the best all-around cowboy or cowgirl, and there were first-place prizes of five hundred dollars in several events. Among those competing, the newspapers listed Bill Pickett, Colonel Zack Mulhall, Emery LaGrande, Ed Lindsey, Slim Caskey, Jim Cahlman, Johnny Baker, Burke Burnett, Jesse Stahl, Mexican Joe, and Hank Durnell. Said the *Chicago Herald*:

In a program of a dozen or more hair-raising ranch stunts the one big thriller is that furnished by the cowboy bull-doggers. . . . This event was won yesterday by "Bill" Pickett in eleven seconds, which is near the world's record. Another thriller was the roping and tying of a steer by Lucille Mulhall, woman champion of the world, in fifty-three seconds.

Famous bucking horses listed were Old Dynamite, valued at $2,000; Death Valley, valued at $10,000; Pancho Villa, valued at $10,000; and Going Wrong, valued at $15,000. Going Wrong had been at Frontier

145

Day celebration contests all over the West and had never been ridden. He was owned by Colonel Idaho Bill and brought from Juarez, Mexico for his Chicago appearance. (Good proven bucking horses are bringing as much as $4,350 today.) It is interesting to note that the bite-'em bulldog hold that Pickett had invented was fading from the scene under the pressure of the humane society and the fact that most cowboys were repulsed at the thought of taking the snotty upper lip of a steer in their mouths. The Chicago rules for the bulldogging event stated, "Positively no biting allowed." The old days were beginning to fade.

Following the Chicago Roundup a four-day Kansas City Roundup was staged by a group of Kansas City men who imported Joe A. Bartles of Dewey, Oklahoma, to manage the big event. This was the first time Bartles had managed a rodeo except the Dewey Roundup which he had been managing since the first one in 1908. The Roundup was scheduled for the first four days in September at Federal League Ball Park, 47th Street and Troost Avenue. It was advertised as a contest in championship elimination events of roping, bulldogging, bronco busting, wild horse racing, trick roping and riding. $10,000 in prize money was offered with prizes from $750 to $2,000 for the four days and day money of $2,500 divided among the various contests. It was reported that the Roundup was staged at a cost of $20,000 with two rodeos daily, afternoons $1, nights 50 cents.

Many of the 350 cowgirls and cowboys who assembled for the Roundup had taken part in the New York "Stampede," the "Frontier Day Celebration" or the

Chicago "Roundup." The following cowboys and cow-girls took part in the contest: Bill Pickett, Jack Fretz, W. H. Hale, Hugo Strickland, Tommy Douglas, J. Ellison Carrol, Ed Henderson, Doc Pardee, Jesse Stahl, George Wier, Eddie Burgess, Harry Walters, Fox Hast-ings, Lucille Mulhall, Louise Thompson, Prairie Rose Henderson, Fanny Sperry Stelle, Helen Maisch and the Irwin sisters, Frances and Edith.

On the opening day, Prairie Rose Henderson, five times world champion woman bronco rider, made a beautiful ride on "Morning Glory," and Harry Walters displayed a brilliant display of horsemanship. The two standouts on the second day were Doc Pardee's winning of the steer roping in 37 seconds and Jesse Stahl's great ride on "Midnight," one of history's great-est bucking horses. The third day had thrills and spills a plenty; many of the roping and dogging steers jumped the low fence around the arena in a futile attempt to go home. Jack Fretz fractured his left leg bulldogging as did W. H. Hale. Bill Pickett lost his hold and the steer he was dogging turned and charged him, knocking him down, scratching, bruising and cutting his face with a horn; however, he was not seriously injured. George Wier won the steer roping with a record time of 25 3/5 seconds. Eddie Burgess placed second with a time of 26 3/5 seconds.

Close on the heels of the Kansas City event came the Cattlemen's Carnival in Garden City, Kansas, from September 7 through September 9, 1916. The attendance was large, and there were contestants from twelve states throughout the nation. *The Wild Bunch* magazine (published at Mulhall, Oklahoma, by Homer

Cattlemen's Carnival, Garden City, Kansas, September 7-9, 1916. It was at this rodeo that Pickett bulldogged his steer in eight seconds. His time was only one second short of the world's record for the year set by Fred Atkinson at the same rodeo. Courtesy The Kansas State Historical Society, Topeka.

Wilson, it carried articles and other information about rodeos and wild west shows throughout the nation) had this to say:

A point worth mention is that we had World Champions in each event. J. H. Strickland, Lee Caldwell, Bugger Red Jr., all hold world championship belts in bronc riding; Prairie Rose Henderson and Catherine Wilks each hold Champion belts in the ladies bronco busting contests. John Murrah, Clay Mc-Gonigal, George and Charley Weir, Henry Grammer, Fred Beeson, Joe Gardner, each hold world championship titles with steer roping. Ed Lindsey and Bill Pickett each hold world championship belts in steer bulldogging. These with many prominent riders and ropers, make up the large list of contestants that took part in the contest.

The stock used in this contest was the best that could be secured. . . . The steers used in the roping contest and in the bulldogging and steer riding were Old Mexico steers secured for this special event. . . .

Bulldogging Contest. Bill Pickett, 1st—time 8 seconds and 12 seconds, $75.00; Fred Atkinson, 2nd—time 7 seconds and 28 seconds, $50.00; Ed Lindsey, 3rd—time 8 3/5 seconds and 59 4/5 seconds, $50.00.

World's Record for 1916 in bulldogging was made here by Fred Atkinson; time 7 seconds.

All in all, the 1916 season was successful, although profits tapered off near the end. The 101 Ranch show made the transition to new ownership, and Bill Pickett returned to the 101 after a very rewarding personal season. He remained there and occupied himself with regular work for the next two years.

Pickett was involved in a tragic accident at Boley, Oklahoma, in August 1918. He was riding his horse down a street when he spotted a friend, Edwin Young, hunkered down changing an automobile tire. He decided to have some fun, so he roped Young as he rode by. Unfortunately, the rope caught Young around the neck, and when Bill's horse tightened up on the rope, Young's neck was broken. He lived only a short time. Bill was heartbroken by the accident and resolved never again to pull that kind of prank on anyone.

Pickett attended a Fourth of July rodeo at Fairfax, Oklahoma, in 1919 and was to bulldog a steer as an exhibition. However, the steer fell hard and died of a broken neck. Ben Johnson and World Champion Steer Roper Henry Grammer performed at the rodeo for a side bet of one thousand dollars to the winner on the average for three steers (Henry Grammer and Bill Hale each put up five hundred dollars to call Lawrence Watson's bet of one thousand dollars). The stakes up, the roping began. Johnson bettered Grammer on the first two steers but failed to throw his third steer, thus giving the win to Grammer on the averages.

↞ IX ↠

TOO OLD
BUT STILL DOGGING

Bill Pickett was now forty-eight and regarded in years as too old to be a bulldogger. He worked at routine cowboy jobs on the 101 Ranch during the war years and up until 1920.

In June 1920, Pickett and another cowboy by the name of Jack M. Smith, a man to whom he had taught the finer points of bulldogging, were working at a line camp on the old Bar L Ranch. (This spread, located east of 101 headquarters, belonged to the Miller brothers and was used to pasture a large herd of cattle.) They acquired a circular announcing the Dewey Roundup, to be held on July 3, 4, and 5 at the new fairgrounds north of Dewey. At this time, it was one of the world's top rodeos, rated with Cheyenne, Pendleton, and Calgary. The first Dewey Roundup was held in 1908 under the management of Joe A. Bartles, who made rodeo history with his custom of paying off the winners in gold, which he carried into the arena in his Stetson. Bill and Jack decided they needed a few days off, and a good rodeo was just the thing to make life worthwhile; besides, there wasn't anything pressing at the ranch. So, without notifying the Millers or anyone else, they saddled up and set out for Dewey. They arrived on the third and paid their entry fees in the bulldogging; Milt Hinkle also was entered. In all events, the prize money was for a three-day average; no day money was offered.

Before a crowd of ten thousand, Pickett finished first in bulldogging on the first day with a time of twenty-four and one-fifth seconds, and Hinkle placed second. Smith also downed his steer. On the second day, Pickett lost his steer and Hinkle finished first; again Smith downed his steer, but not in record time. Fifteen thousand people watched. July 5 dawned bright and clear, and by the time the bulldogging began, the temperature was 100 degrees and not a breath of air was stirring. Pickett again turned in the best time for the day, and Hinkle came in second. Smith's turn arrived, and he looked with some apprehension upon the steer he had drawn: a big, wild Brahma-Longhorn cross with long, thin, sharp horns. He spoke to Pickett about his dislike for the animal; Bill told him that if he were afraid of the steer, he should never attempt to bulldog it because that was just asking for an accident.

Smith did not heed the warning. Instead, he signaled for the steer to be turned loose. The brute came out strong, and as it crossed the barrier, Smith was after him with perfect timing. He rode up beside the steer in what appeared to be record time, latched onto the steer's horns, and brought him to a stop in short order. The steer had a rubber neck, and Smith was having a hard time twisting it down; his sweaty hand slipped from the beast's right horn. The steer kept pawing and lunging until Smith lost his hold and fell to the ground on his back. The enraged steer backed off a few yards, lowered his head, and lunged at Smith's prostrate body. One of the horns pierced Smith's right side and he was tossed high, his intestines trailing onto the maddened animal's horns. The steer came at him a second time but was discouraged when Smith kicked at him (Smith continued until help arrived). Pickett jumped on his horse and drove the steer away from the cowboy. Smith was carefully placed in an ambulance by his friends, but he was dead before it could pull out of the arena. Fifteen thousand people witnessed the tragic event.

Milt Hinkle, who placed second, first, and second during the three days, was awarded first in bulldogging on the three-day average; Pickett was second. Pickett also rode with others in the multiple roping, won by Homer Wilson. Blue Gentry turned in a record time of twenty-four and one-fifth seconds in the steer roping on the Fourth of July. Skeeter Bill Robbins gave an exhibition of fancing roping, and Madd Tarr, Mildred Hinkle, and Dorothy Robbins put on a real show in the cowgirl wild horse riding.

Pickett's time of 24.2 seconds seems terribly slow alongside Oral Harris Zumwalt's world record time of 2.2 seconds. However, there are official records that credit Pickett with a time of 8 seconds flat. In 1914, Sam Garrett won the bulldogging at Pendleton in 25.4 seconds. Today, anything under 10 seconds is considered good. Time is affected considerably by the size of the arena, the rules governing the length of the starting barrier, and the size of the steers used. Some rodeos turn out the steer lap and tap, which means bulldogger and steer leave the chute simultaneously; some set a 10-foot, 20-foot, or even 50-foot barrier, which means the steer is given that much of a lead before the starting flag is dropped. The weight of the dogging steers used now is limited: minimum 400 pounds, maximum 750 pounds. In Pickett's day, they weighed anywhere from 800 to 1,100 pounds, with most on the heavy side of these weights, and they were wild and mean. Nor did the first bulldoggers use a hazer as is done today.

Pickett gave a bulldogging exhibition at the 1920 rodeo in Sand Springs, Oklahoma. He missed his first steer and plowed up the ground with his head. His face was a bloody mess. After being bandaged up until only his eyes were visible, he returned to the arena, asked for another steer, and downed it without incident. In recognition of his grit, the audience showered him with coins; the rodeo was held up while Pickett gathered them.

Bill Pickett did indeed bulldog steers with his hands tied behind his back. It sounds impossible, but with his experience and ability, it wasn't so hard for him. The way it was accomplished seemed quite simple to Bill. He jumped from his horse and proceeded to stop the steer as usual, turned his head and elevated the nose, clamped his teeth into the upper lip, and held the steer while an assistant tied Bill's hands behind him. Then, hands securely bound, Bill would simply throw his weight onto the lip and topple the animal, falling with it and holding his grip all the while. He would hold the downed animal with his teeth until the crowd was satisfied, then simply turn loose and roll free, or perhaps have an assistant help free him. Old-time cowboys say that bulldogged steers, once they had regained their feet, would never attack Pickett. One can assume the animals had had enough of the Dusky Demon by this time.

Pickett estimated in 1930 that, during his lifetime, he had bulldogged some five thousand head of cattle, mostly steers. This is not far fetched when one considers that for years he bulldogged twice daily with the 101 Ranch Show and that on some days he would dog more than one steer at each performance. From existing records and personal accounts, it has been established that Bill Pickett was a contestant in bulldogging events at the following rodeos or roundups and actually competed for prize money: Ardmore, Oklahoma; Wichita Falls, Texas; Comanche, Oklahoma; Fort Worth, Texas; Pawnee, Oklahoma; Dewey, Oklahoma (1920-21-22); Silverdale, Kansas; Vinita, Oklahoma; Winfield, Kansas; Omaha, Nebraska (1916); rodeos held at the 101 Ranch; New York Stampede, August 6-13, 1916; Chicago Roundup, August 19-27, 1916; Kansas City Roundup, September 1-4, 1916; Cattlemen's Carnival, Garden City, Kansas, September 7-9, 1916. Pickett would have been a contestant at many more rodeos between 1910 and 1930 had it not been for the color line at many of them, both large and small. This restricted his activities and prevented him from compiling a better record as a bulldogger, bronc rider, and steer and calf roper.

After the 1920 Dewey Roundup, Pickett returned to the 101 Ranch for a short time, then moved with his family to Oklahoma City. While living there, he worked first at the Oklahoma City Stockyards as a drover and later for the Southwestern Oil Mill Company as a mill hand. Maggie and the girls were happy to have him working regular hours and coming home each night instead of being gone for long stretches on the show circuit. Bill was not so content; he longed for ranch life and the roar of the crowds at rodeos. He missed the smell of sweaty men, horses, and cattle and the dust and mud of the arena, as well as his association with the 101 Ranch cowhands and the Miller brothers. The new life that was so acceptable to Bill's family gradually became drudgery for him. His only contacts with the old life were the few round-ups he attended.

Bill made the Dewey Roundup in 1921 and 1922 and was a contestant in the bulldogging contests. He also competed at the Winfield, Kansas, rodeo in June 1921. In the bulldogging event, a pair of hand-made boots was offered as the prize. There was a 60-foot barrier, and the arena was very wet and muddy after several days of heavy rains. There were four contestants: Pickett, Guy Schultz, Paddy Ryan, and Jim Ballew. Schultz and Ryan missed their steers and registered no time. Pickett piled off onto his animal, but the steer ducked his head under Bill's weight and Bill lost his footing and went down. Pickett was thrown clear. He immediately regained his feet, grabbed the

The 101 Ranch Wild West Show performers as they appeared in New York, July 22–August 5, 1928. Bill Pickett is sitting in the upper right. Courtesy Beth Ray, *Yale News*, Yale, Oklahoma.

steer as it struggled to get up, and dogged the animal but his time was very poor. Jim Ballew was more fortunate than the others and got his steer on his first try in 22 seconds.

After the event Pickett advised Ballew that he had been lucky and that he had better get some more practice before attempting to dog big, wild steers or he would get himself killed as Jack Smith did at Dewey the year before. Jim took the advice and never bulldogged again. He also sold his prize boots to George Bacon Rind, an Osage Indian, for forty-five dollars and later remarked that the mud and wear and tear on his gear was worth more than that.

After four years of part-time absence from the 101 Ranch, Bill Pickett returned in 1924 for keeps. During the years that followed, he was not on the regular payroll, but simply went to the Millers when he needed money and drew whatever his immediate needs required. Times were hard during his last hitch at the ranch, and money was hard to come by, even for the Miller organization.

Pickett participated in two rodeos at the ranch in 1924: August 31 and Labor Day. Florence Reynolds, a cowgirl bronc rider who was a contestant at both of these contests, said of him: "Pickett was a great bulldogger and pickup man. I wouldn't have anyone else pick me off a bronc. He was a good kind person. I visited with him several times. . . . Everybody on the ranch liked Bill. He didn't talk much."

ʁ **X** ʁ

LIFE
AND A NEW 101 SHOW

In the winter of 1924-25, the Miller brothers bought the Walter L. Main Circus, lock, stock, and barrel. They planned to combine it with the new wild west show they were putting together at the ranch. The rest of the winter was spent in preparing the show for its spring opening in Oklahoma City on April 21, 1925.

During the winter, Bill Pickett practiced bulldogging and looked forward with great anticipation to the upcoming season with the new show. Maggie was less enthusiastic, for she had treasured every moment of the last eight years (except for the rodeo tours) that Bill had been home with her and the girls. She resented his going on the road again and hated to see the routine of their life disrupted. Even more bothersome than the resentment, however, was the gnawing fear, ever a shadow in her life, that Bill would be injured or killed while bulldogging. The girls were not so apprehensive; they were old enough to enjoy the renown and prestige their father had gained, as well as pride of being Bill Pickett's daughters. They mingled with the performers as they watched the many preparations for the new show.

One of Joe Miller's stage properties was his new saddle, which he used in parades and the grand entry. He had seen Napoleon's saddle in Paris while the show was touring Europe, and a museum guide had told him it was the most expensive in the world. Right then and there, Joe decided to outdo Napoleon — and did. His saddle cost a little more than five thousand dollars, and 210 diamonds, rubies, and sapphires were used as ornaments. *Joseph C. Miller* was spelled out in 168 diamonds. Eight pounds of solid gold and silver were used in finishing off this saddle to end all saddles. It was a thing of great beauty and workmanship and attracted the attention of the public as it was intended to do. Joe's saddle was a far cry from the well-worn stock saddle Bill Pickett used in his bulldogging act. It was plain but well kept, much worn from hard use; it was the sturdy saddle of a working cowhand. The gems of Bill's saddle were the many hundreds of successful leaps he made from it through the years as he dogged steers.

One of the attractions for visitors to the 101 Ranch was a cage of monkeys and a large brown bear named Tony. Both were near the store where ranch products and soft drinks were sold to the public and ranch personnel. During his lifetime, Tony drank hundreds of bottles of soda pop and became a huge animal. Pickett had a very interesting experience with him in connection with a movie filmed on the ranch. Tony was to be used in the movie, and Bill Pickett was delegated to haul him to the set. However, Tony had other ideas about riding in a truck and refused to get in. Wes Rogers, the ranch foreman, came out to help load the bear. He and Bill pushed and tugged on Tony, tried to tempt him with food, threatened him, and cussed him, all to no avail. Tony simply refused to budge. Finally, in desperation, Wes roped Tony and pulled while Bill pushed. Still no soap. As a last resort, Wes mounted his horse and took a dally with the rope around the saddle horn, rode around in front of the truck, and began to pull on the bear. Tony decided he had had enough of this foolishness and lunged up into the truck. But instead of stopping in the bed, he plunged forward through the cloth back of the truck cab and wound up inside the cab with Pickett. The bear and the cowboy filled the cab to overflowing, but after sizing up the situation, Bill put the truck into gear and, a wide grin on his face, took off for the movie set. He arrived with his wild cargo without further incident.

The Miller Brothers' 101 Ranch Real Wild West and Great Far East Show was launched on schedule in Oklahoma City. The opening performance was dedicated to the celebration commemorating the opening of Oklahoma Territory in 1889. Tom S. Tucker, widely known show organizer, had been hired by Joe Miller to put it all together, for Joe meant business to make the show the best and told Tucker to spend whatever was necessary to obtain results.

The new enterprise was valued at three hundred thousand dollars, and old showmen said there was never a show on the road with such wagons and railroad cars as those used by the Millers. Skilled work-men were hired at top wages. A large building in Marland, Oklahoma, was rented, and machinery was brought in to handle the special construction work. Some forty new wagons were built. The thirty rail-road cars, most of them of steel, were constructed in Marland, as were the cars housing performers and other employees. All were the best money could buy. The private car used by the Millers as their home on the road was a palace on wheels: private baths, electric lights, even a library.

Everything in the show was new except the sides of the bandwagon, which were made up of two life-size wood engravings executed years before by a long-forgotten German woodcarver. These pieces of art represented *The Aztec Sacrifice* and *The Landing of Ponce de Leon,* and nowhere in the world could they be equaled.

The big top and arena walls, almost twice as large as the old show had been, were spun from the long-staple cotton grown on the ranch. The wagons, bleach-ers, and other wooden equipment were made of tim-ber processed in the ranch mill. The cook wagons (their refrigeration boxes could hold a two-day supply of ice) were marvels of construction; less than an hour after they arrived on the lot, meals for the entire troupe were ready. By its very nature and the dreams of the Miller brothers, the show truly represented the real Wild West. Every cowboy, cowgirl, roper, bronco buster, bulldogger, every man or woman who fired a gun, was an admitted champion. Zack Miller was in charge of the show, and no one was better experienced or equipped by nature to carry out the task.

The Far East segment of the show featured fourteen hundred people from all nations, three hundred Indians, six hundred horses, and scores of wild animals. Trains of refrigerated cars left for the show site every ten days with thirty thousand pounds of meat, fruit and vegetables for the mess-tent tables.

The new show didn't do well financially, in spite of the fact that it received enthusiastic approval from the public. It encountered the stiffest competition any business ever had: Barnum & Bailey, the Ringlings, and the American Circus Corporation. The 101 performers held their own with the public, but the show's income declined to such an extent that the 1926 season closed with a loss of about $119,000. Bad business conditions and increased production costs forced the show off the road in 1931.

In the 1920's, the Miller brothers promoted a bulldogging exhibition at a theater in the 300 block of East Grand Avenue in Ponca City. Owned by Mr. and Mrs. H. C. R. Brodboll, the theater was Ponca City's finest. The exhibition was billed as a featured performance by Bill Pickett, who would attempt to bulldog a steer on the stage. Admission was five cents for children, ten cents for adults. Pickett was successful, and the act ran several days. In one performance, the audience was given something extra for its money in the form of a good scare when Pickett's steer jumped off the stage and went charging wildly up the main aisle. No one was injured.

On June 1, 1926, Bill had a little run-in with the law in Kay County. The county attorney issued a warrant charging him with possession of choc beer (an Indian beverage with a milky color—hence the name *choc beer*—that was especially popular among Indians and Negroes in Oklahoma during Prohibition). The affair was the result of a raid on Pickett's house at the 101 Ranch following gunplay by some blacks who had gathered there. The sheriff was called, and he alleged that Pickett had turned bootlegger (cowboys who were at the ranch at this time have told me that Pickett was a good consumer of choc beer but was never a bootlegger). Bill appeared before Judge J. L. Roberson and was arraigned; he pleaded innocent, and bond was set at one thousand dollars. It can be assumed that he was put in jail until June 7, at which time he filed bond. It was approved, trial was set for November 27. On November 19, he entered a plea of guilty, was found guilty, and was fined twenty-five dollars and costs.

Bill's white friends tell me they never saw him drunk, although he drank all his life and a half-pint was an average drink for him. His theory was to take a good stiff drink and then not drink any more until it began to take effect, then take another stiff one if needed. In this way, he reasoned, one would never become drunk. His friends drank with him and from his bottle. It was his custom to let the white cowboys drink directly from the bottle first; then he would pour himself a drink into a clean Prince Albert tobacco tin he carried for that purpose. In this way, he could avoid any criticism regarding whites and blacks drinking from the same bottle. Bill was always regarded by the cowboys as sociable and polite and

Probably the last picture taken of Bill Pickett. He loved cigars and red shirts.

was well liked by everyone, although he was willful and had his own ideas about things. His children say he did not care to associate with Negroes, preferring the company of white people. This was due in part to the fact that he had been employed by white men and most of the employees on ranches, in wild west shows, and at rodeos were, with few exceptions, white. His stature as a headliner and his close association with white employers and cowboys contributed to a certain amount of jealousy among his fellow blacks. As in the choc beer incident, Bill was plagued by his black friends all his life. They would move in on him and stay until all his food and liquor were exhausted and he could not borrow any more from his white friends. Such people caused Bill a great deal of trouble, especially in his later years and after Maggie's death.

In 1927, the Miller brothers built a monument to the memory of Chief White Eagle in the triangle pasture just south of the old buffalo pasture. The site is a high hill in Noble County three miles southeast of ranch headquarters. The monument, of red sandstone, was five feet in diameter and fourteen feet high and was topped with a white stone eagle. A marble tablet near the base was inscribed:

> Indian Trail Marker
> Re-erected to the memory of
> Chief White Eagle (1840-1914)
> Who led his people to civilization
> And favored the White Man's ways
> Erected by Miller Brothers
> 101 Ranch, June 1927

The dedication was attended by the Millers, Bill Pickett, and most of the cowboys at the ranch, as well as various friends and the curious from near and far. All of the living Ponca chiefs and many visiting chiefs from other tribes were on hand. Horse Chief Eagle presided, and a prayer to the Great Spirit was recited by Head Walker. The monument was unveiled by White Eagle's granddaughter, Elaine Waters, and his aged widow, Victoria.

The monument was a guidepost like those erected by Plains Indians throughout Oklahoma, Kansas and

Nebraska. They were placed on hills so that they were visible for great distances. Tribal and intertribal messages were left there, spelled out in twigs, sand, and rocks.

Bill was still a working cowboy on the 101 Ranch in February 1928 when he nearly joined his ancestors. As he was riding his horse across a cornfield just east of the apple orchard (two miles directly east of ranch headquarters), he saw a coyote and gave chase. He took down his rope and built a loop as the horse followed the coyote at full speed. Bill dropped his loop over the coyote and was ready to haul it in when his horse stepped in a gopher hole, turned a double somersault, broke its neck, and landed squarely across Pickett's body, pinning him underneath in such a position that he could not extricate himself. He said later: "The whole thing happened so quickly that it was all over before I hardly knew what was happening. I was afraid the horse would kick me, as my head was not very far from his heels. I managed to raise up his head while he was still breathing, I could tell that he was dying, then I was afraid he would kick during his death struggles. Luckily, he didn't."

After working for quite a while, Bill realized he could not free himself, and he began calling for help. More than an hour later, he attracted the attention of some people who lived near by, and they summoned some passing Santa Fe section hands. The gandy dancers lifted the dead horse off Pickett's body and released him, none the worse for his ordeal. In the meantime, the coyote escaped from the rope and disappeared into the apple orchard.

Colonel Zack T. Miller, youngest of the three Miller brothers and the last to try to salvage the 101 Ranch.

ʁ **XI** ʅ

END OF A COWBOY
AND AN ERA

March 14, 1929, was a dark day in Bill Pickett's life: he lost Maggie. She died in a hospital after a short illness and is buried near Norman, Oklahoma. Life was never quite the same for Bill after Maggie's death. He drank too much and moved into a small house at 101 headquarters from the large white house (east of Marland on the road to the Bar L Ranch) in which he and Maggie had lived since 1924. It was the same house they had occupied before moving to Oklahoma City in 1920. Bill remembered well the many times Maggie had pleaded with him to give up bulldogging; she was sure that in the end, he would be killed. He was injured many times, and most of the bones in his body were cracked or broken during a very active thirty years of rough-and-tumble life, but he was still alive.

During the late 1920's and early 1930's the 101 Ranch encountered very dark days. Joe Miller's death in 1927 (he was the victim of carbon monoxide gas in his garage) was a severe blow to the enterprise because his guiding hand was firm and steady. In 1929, George Miller was killed in an automobile accident on an icy road as he returned to the ranch from Ponca City. He was the financial wizard and efficient manager of the spread, a shrewd man and an irreplaceable asset to the ranch. Dan Feary, the manager of the ranch store, opined that "the mind and spirit of the 101 Ranch was dead." The management of the 101 Ranch fell to Zack Miller and Joe's sons, George W., and Joe C., Jr.

In 1929, the bottom fell out of everything: the oil business, the cattle business, agriculture, and horticulture, and the Miller empire was caught in the grasp of the Great Depression. The Millers felt that the economic squeeze was only temporary, and to tide them over, they borrowed more than $500,000. Things worsened in 1930, and by the end of the year, the ranch had suffered a loss of $301,064.08. Interest, taxes, notes, and mortgages became due, then past due, and there were no funds to pay the many creditors. The ranch had vast stores of oil, hay, and grain, as well as cattle, but there was no market for them and therefore no income. Zack hoped that the show would bring in the needed cash during the 1931 season. However, bad luck and poor management plagued it and it folded in Washington, D.C., in August and was shipped back to the ranch, never to take the road again. Even then, it was only by a stroke of luck and a court order that the show returned home.

In November, 1931, the ranch was in debt to the tune of $626,762.33 but had assets appraised at $1,873.674.00. Earlier, on September 16, 1931, Judge

John S. Burger of Kay County District Court had confirmed the appointment of Fred C. Clarke, a rancher from Winfield, Kansas, as general operating receiver. On that day, the 101 Ranch passed from the Millers' control. Then began plans to dispose of the 101's real property and certain pieces of real estate in an effort to salvage at least part of the ranch.

Bill Pickett worked at the ranch during these critical days, doing anything he could to help save what he had called home for most of a quarter century. Zack Miller always maintained that Pickett knew, individually, every head of livestock on the ranch. On March 15, 1932, a horse buyer arrived, and Zack showed him some horses broken to the saddle. There was one old show horse that had been a bucker but had quit bucking. The buyer liked its looks and asked Zack to have someone saddle and ride it. Miller delegated Pickett to the chore. Bill saddled up and stepped aboard. The old outlaw must have decided to have one more fling because he gave Pickett the ride of his life. The Dusky Demon rode the horse to a standstill with all the style and finesse of his youth.

After lunch four days later, Red Taggart, livestock manager at the 101, ordered Bill Pickett, Jack Berkley, and Walton Lewis, who were in charge of livestock, to get a bunch of horses ready for the upcoming liquidation sale. The assignment meant having the horses at least halter broken so that they could be sold at halter. Just before starting the afternoon's work, Pickett, in the company of Lewis, purchased some choc beer from a black bootlegger. Lewis noted that Bill had quite a roll of bills in his old wallet when he paid

171

Walton Lewis, Bill Pickett's saddle buddy and friend in the early 1930's. Walton worked with him on the day of his fatal accident and was the last to hear his voice.

for the beer. Bill took several stiff snorts of the stuff before he and Lewis rode down to the large training corral, some three hundred yards southwest of the ranch store, to begin working the horses.

The corral, about one and a half acres in size, previously had been used to train horses for the 101 Ranch show. On this particular day, it held about 125 head of horses, some of them very wild and unbroken. Lewis Patrick Tucker, Negro ranch hand and boxer with the ranch sideshow for several seasons, was one of several ranch employees and visitors who were present that afternoon to watch the action in the corral (Tucker verified the day's events years later at his home in Oklahoma City). Pickett was mounted on a very fine, 1,000-pound white cutting horse named Hornet, and Lewis rode an equally good 1,050-pound animal, white with blue ticking, called Blue. (A cutting horse does just that: cuts horses or cattle out of a herd. When he begins his work, he is made to understand which animal is wanted, and he works quietly until that animal is moved to the edge of the herd. He requires no assistance from his rider.) Baldy, Savanna, and Croppie were Pickett's later dogging horses, all of which were in his string of mounts but were the property of the ranch.

The first horse Pickett elected to separate from the herd was a three-year-old chestnut gelding, wild, mean, unbroken, and weighing about one thousand pounds. He was all horse and as wicked as they come. This was probably the reason Pickett selected him because Bill loved to display his prowess in whatever the job at hand. He tied his rope to the saddle horn, rode into the herd, and flipped his loop over the chestnut's head. The fight began. Bill dallied his rope around the saddle horn and began to take up the slack as he worked the chestnut toward Hornet. Just as the horse was nearly close enough to reach, he made a mighty lunge and Bill was unable to hold him, the rope shooting out of his hands. Angered by the actions of the horse, Pickett jumped from his mount and began to approach the chestnut hand over hand down the rope. The other horses began to snort and run around the inside of the corral fence.

By this time, a number of ranch hands and visitors had assembled atop the fence to watch the show. Finally, one of the running horses stepped on Pickett's rope, making it slack for an instant, and the rope flipped up and caught Pickett just as the chestnut hit the other end. Bill was tossed about fifteen feet into the air, and when he landed, it was behind and near the chestnut. Instantly, the horse kicked Bill in the head with the left hind foot, making a sound not unlike that heard when a ripe melon is squashed. Pickett quickly got up and stood hunched over with his hands on his knees, blood gushing from his mouth, nose, and ears. Walton Lewis jumped from his horse and ran to Bill's aid, arriving just as Pickett lost consciousness and collapsed into his arms.

The accident had occurred in less than a minute. Lewis yelled for someone to get a car so that Pickett could be rushed to the hospital in Ponca City. He removed Bill's spurs and gave them to Red Taggart, who arrived seconds after the accident. A visitor whose blue 1931 Pierce Arrow roadster was parked near the corral volunteered to drive Pickett to Ponca City. Bill was carefully laid in Lewis' arms in the front seat, and the driver took off in a cloud of dust, nearly losing both Pickett and Lewis as he whirled the car around and headed north. The car door flew open; Lewis saw something fly out but thought nothing of it in the excitement of the moment. Someone had called ahead, and as the car pulled up to the hospital doorway, Dr. Araedell, an orderly, and a nun were waiting. When the doctor saw who the patient was, he said: "Ah, hell, it's Pickett. He'll live." Bill had been in and out of the Ponca City hospital many times before and had always survived.

When Pickett's possessions were checked at the hospital, his wallet was missing. Lewis returned to the ranch and learned that someone had turned the wallet in, empty, at the ranch office. It was the wallet, then, that had flipped out of the car as it took off for the hospital.

Bill Pickett never regained cousciousness. He hovered between life and death for the next fourteen days. On April 2, 1932, the world's best-known bull-dogger died.

When Zack Miller received word that Pickett was dead, he ordered Shorty Corin, the ranch carpenter and blacksmith, to build a box in which to bury the old cowhand. When ranch receiver Fred C. Clarke heard of the homemade coffin, he told Zack Miller to save it for himself. Bill Pickett, Clarke said, was to have a proper casket and burial, which would be provided by a Ponca City funeral home, and he, Clarke, had personally made all of the arrangements,

175

which would be paid for with ranch funds. That, Clarke said, was the least anyone could do for a cowboy who had worked for the 101 Ranch the most of his adult life.

Zack Miller announced that the funeral would be held at the 101 Ranch on the porch of the White House at 3:00 p.m. Sunday, April 3 (Joe Miller had been buried from the same place). The funeral was postponed until Tuesday, April 5, however, so that Bill's daughter Bessie, who lived in Chicago, could attend the service. Alberta, who lived in Omaha, Nebraska, did not know of her father's death and funeral until noon on the fifth. She was listening to a Will Rogers radio broadcast when Rogers announced that Pickett was to be buried that afternoon on the 101 Ranch. He also remarked that Bill was a close friend, that he had known him for many years, and that he had great admiration for the Negro cowboy. On many occasions, Rogers said, he had enjoyed the hospitality of Bill and Maggie Pickett in their home.

The funeral service was conducted by the Reverend S. Sylvester Fairley of St. John's Baptist Church in Ponca City, who brought the church choir to sing hymns. It was a large funeral, attended by Indians, cowboys, ranch hands, farmers, people from Ponca City, and members of Pickett's family. In all, several hundred people were there, and more than ninety per cent of them were white. Many eyes were wet. After the service, the funeral procession moved south of the ranch three miles to the site of the White Eagle monument, where a brief committal service was held

Bill Pickett's last resting place in the triangle pasture of the 101 Ranch, near the monument to Ponca Indian Chief White Eagle. The initials stand for the Cherokee Strip Cowpunchers Association, who paid for the gravestone.

and the choir sang *Swing Low, Sweet Chariot* as the coffin was lowered into the grave.

Zack Miller announced that Bill Pickett's dogging horse, Croppie, would be sold and the proceeds used to erect a fitting marker on Pickett's grave. However, this was not accomplished in the way Miller had planned. The Cherokee Strip Cowpunchers Association, of which Pickett was the only black member, erected a sandstone marker on September 6, 1936, with this simple inscription: BILL PICKETT, C. S. C. A.

As the crow flies, Bill Pickett's grave is one and one-half miles south of the Kay County line in Noble County, Buffalo Township; three miles south of the old 101 Ranch headquarters on the east side of U.S. 77; and a quarter-mile east of the highway. It is fifty feet west of the White Eagle monument and about a half-mile north of the south boundary of the old 101 Ranch property. There is a historical marker on the highway at the south boundary of the ranch, about three-fourths of a mile southwest of the grave. Rocks from a soapstone formation are arranged along the length of the grave on each side, and sage is growing in the rock formation around the grave. The soil is not very fertile on this the highest knoll in the surrounding area, and the ground slopes sharply off to the north in the direction of the Salt Fork of the Arkansas.

Pickett is not alone on this high, wind-swept Oklahoma hill, There are four other graves near by, all 101 Ranch people. Buried here are James E. Smedley, better known as Curbstone Curby, the ox-team trainer and driver with the 101 Ranch show for many years; Henry Clay, a Negro cowboy who taught rope tricks to Will Rogers in his youth; Gladys Hamilton, the nine-year-old daughter of Negro ranch hand Rhyne Hamilton; and Jim Gates, a Negro farm hand who was shot to death at a dance. All of the burials were made in the 1930's, and none has been made since. Bill's best-known bulldogging horse, Spradley, is reported to be buried near by.

Zack Miller dedicated a poem to Bill Pickett on the day Bill died. He sent copies to all his friends, saying he had been Bill's friend and boss for thirty years. Wrote Zack:

OLD BILL IS DEAD

Old Bill has died and gone away,
Over the "Great Divide."
Gone to a place where the preachers says
Both saint and sinner will abide.
If they "check his brand" like I think they will
It's a running hoss they'll give to Bill.
And some good wild steers till he gets his fill.
With a great big crowd for him a thrill.
Bill's hide was black but his heart was white,
He'd sit up through the coldest night
To help a "doggie" in a dyin' fight,
To save a dollar for his boss.
And all Bill wanted was a good fast hoss,
Three square meals and a place to lay
His tired self at the end of day.
There's one other thing, since I've come to think
Bill was always willing to take a drink.
If the job was tough, be it hot or cold,
You could get it done if Bill was told.
He'd fix the fence, or skin a cow,

179

Or ride a bronc, and EVEN PLOW,
Or do anything, if you told him how.
Like many men in the old-time West,
On any job, he did his best.
He left a blank that's hard to fill
For there'll never be another Bill.
Both White and Black will mourn the day
That the "Biggest Boss" took Bill away.

Many other folks also had something to say about
Bill. Will Rogers: "Bill Pickett never had an enemy;
even the steers wouldn't hurt old Bill." C. A. Dill,
an employee of the 101 Ranch in the 1930's: "I know
that I liked him and respected him more than many
white people. He was as loyal and faithful I think as
it would be possible for anyone to be. As far as I know,
he had the respect and liking of everyone who knew
him." Homer Croy, western writer: "Everyone treated
Bill Pickett with great respect, for he was not only
a good man, but he contributed more to rodeo entertainment than any other one person."

Floyd Randolph and Walter Schultz, both old-time
cowboys and wild-west-show performers, made a sin-
cere, affectionate, but racist statement about Bill: "If
there was ever a good nigger, it was Bill Pickett."
Said Zack Miller in a somewhat similar vein: "If there
was a white Negro, it was Bill. His hide was black,
but his heart was white. If all white men had been as
honest and loyal as this Negro, the world wouldn't
be in the shape it's in today." Milt Hinkle: "I was a
close friend of Bill Pickett and worked with him on
and off from 1905 until his tragic death in 1932. Yes,
Bill and I were cowhands, contestants, and wild west
performers together and a finer man and better friend

could not be found. Pickett's skin was black but his heart was as white and pure as any white man's." Walton Lewis, Pickett's long-time friend and sidekick: "Bill Pickett was absolutely without fear regardless of the job at hand." Fred Beeson, thirty-four years a rodeo cowboy, said: "Bill Pickett was a real cowboy. He could bulldog, bronc ride, was a fair roper and could do anything on the ranch that a cowhand was expected to do."

Only a few of the old ranch crew remained on the 101: Zack Miller; Selma Zimmerman, the elephant girl with the wild west show; Harley, a houseboy who had once been on the show staff; and a handful of cowboys and ranch hands. They were soon to be scattered as the ranch was broken up. The good old days were over, and the 101 Ranch was an institution of the past. It was the end of an era never to be repeated in the American West.

EPILOGUE

As these words are written, the spirit and courage of Bill Pickett and the pride with which he viewed his profession live on in a great-grandson, Willie Wilson of Spencer, Oklahoma, who is a rodeo cowboy. It is more than a hobby with him, for his record reveals many wins in his chosen work. Like Great-Grandfather Bill, Willie is a bulldogger, a man of whom Bill would be mighty proud if the Dusky Demon were alive.

Bill Pickett has not been forgotten. One of his greatest admirers, Gareth Muchmore, editor of the *Ponca City News*, has suggested that it would befit the memory of this great cowboy to move his remains from the lonely wind swept hill near the White Eagle monument to Cowboy Hill Cemetery near the Salt Fork of the Arkansas. Here are buried Zack Miller, the last of the Miller brothers; Jack Webb, billed by the 101 Ranch Wild West Show as "America's most sensational trick, fancy rifle and pistol shot"; and Sam

C. Stigall, foreman of the 101 Ranch from 1902 to 1929. The plot, a gift from the Miller brothers to the Cherokee Strip Cowpunchers Association, lies on the south bluff of the Salt Fork, south of the old ranch headquarters, on Oklahoma State Highway 156; it is just east of the river bridge. A better resting place could not be found, for here the wind whispers through the river willows and the grass is green and lush. Perhaps Bill Pickett soon will lie here among friends, for response to Muchmore's suggestions has been favorable.

It is surprising to note how many of Bill's personal articles have been preserved by his friends and admirers through the years. Perhaps the most valuable is his saddle, although it has no silver or gold mountings or elaborate decorations. It is well worn, and its scuff marks testify that it was indeed a working cowboy's saddle. It was owned by Sonny Schultz of Ponca City, Oklahoma, a nephew of Guy Schultz. Guy, well known as a bronco buster for the 101 Ranch, developed the gentle art of bulldogging buffalo. He and Bill were the closest of friends and shared many heartaches and joys in their dangerous work. Schultz promised to give the saddle to the National Rodeo Cowboy Hall of Fame if and when Bill Pickett was voted into its membership and provided the saddle was placed on public exhibition.

I have recently acquired the bridle bit Bill used on Spradley during the 101 Ranch Wild West Show's tour of Mexico in 1908. The bit is a plain U.S. Cavalry issue, just like the ones that a thousand other cowboys used after the Civil War because they were cheap and easy to come by. Riveted to the mouth bar is a silver plate inscribed as follows:

Used by Bill Pickett in First Public Demonstration of Bull-dogging Mexico City, Christmas Eve 1908.

The engraving probably was ordered by Joe Miller, and the bit was probably used in connection with show advertising and retained later at the 101 White House as a mememto of Bill's exploits in the bull ring at Mexico City. It is my wish that the bit become part of a Bill Pickett Collection to be enjoyed by the general public.

The National Rodeo Cowboy Hall of Fame is part of the National Cowboy Hall of Fame and Western Heritage Center at Oklahoma City. Annually, it recognizes the All-Around Champion of the Rodeo Cowboys Association in Denver, and the winner is enshrined as World Champion Cowboy for that year. In the forty-four years of official records kept by the association, twenty-seven cowboys have won this coveted award. Some of the champions have won it two, three, or four times. Oklahoma's Jim Shoulders has won it five times and Larry Mahan six.

Until 1971, National Rodeo Cowboy Hall of Fame Honorees were deceased white cowboys who had left their mark on the rodeo profession. One Honoree was and is selected each year by the Board of Trustees of the National Cowboy Hall of Fame from nominations submitted by the Rodeo Historical Society, which in turn distributes ballots to its members. The Honorees are primarily cowboys who performed their daring feats before official records were kept (beginning in 1929) by the Rodeo Cowboys Association.

Bill Pickett was nominated as an Honoree to the National Rodeo Cowboy Hall of Fame in 1969; he placed third in the balloting. He was renominated in 1970 by me and tied for second place.

In 1970, a new rule was adopted by the Board of Trustees: All nominees are to be placed on the ballot for three years or until elected, and at the end of the three-year period, all nominees were eligible for renomination for three more years or until elected. (Each year, there are fifteen to twenty nominations.) The Board of Trustees is not bound by this rule, but it is the board's usual practice to elect the nominee of the Rodeo Historical Society, who is in turn nominated by the Rodeo Cowboys Association.

In 1971, there were twenty nominees, and Eddie Curtis of Nowata, Oklahoma, was elected. Bill Pickett was a close second. Said Sam Garrett: "Bill Pickett was a great cowboy. I worked with him in 1905 at the 101 Ranch. If ever any one was entitled to be a member of the Cowboy Hall of Fame it is Bill Pickett." Floyd Randolph opined: "Bill Pickett should have been in the Rodeo Cowboy Hall of Fame long ago and if he had been a white man he would have been one of the first."

In 1971, the Board of Trustees again made a rule change. They decided to take in only one Honoree each year but to vote on the Nominees in October, then hold a runoff among the three receiving the most votes. Their thinking was that this would make it possible to elect the Honoree just before the National Finals Rodeo; the announcement and induction could be made during the rodeo.

Under the new rule, Bill Pickett was voted on a second time in 1971. In November, he was elected Honoree for 1972 by the largest majority any nominee had received up to that time, defeating two worthy runnerups: Verne Elliott and Mike Hastings (another bulldogger).

On Thursday, December 9, 1971, at the evening performance of the National Finals Rodeo, Bill Pickett was inducted into the National Rodeo Cowboy Hall of Fame by western film star Joel McCrea. A certificate was presented to Willie Wilson, Bill's great-grandson. Pickett became the twentieth Honoree and the first and only black cowboy awarded a niche in the National Cowboy Hall of Fame and Western Heritage Center in any category.

Immediately after the induction, Sonny Schultz delivered Bill's saddle, now restored, to the Western Heritage Shrine, where it was put on display. Pickett's case is well arranged, with the saddle serving as the center of attention, as is the pattern in other Honorees' displays. A full-length photograph of the Dusky Demon also is on display, along with a good biography of the inventor of bulldogging. In all, it is a worthy tribute to a great cowboy.

BIBLIOGRAPHY

Books

Branch, Hettye Wallace. *The Story of 80 John.* New York, Greenwich Book Publishers Inc., 1960.

Bright, Roderick. *Toras Without Tears.* Mexico 1, D.F., Edeciones Luna, 1949.

Bryson, Dr. J. Gordon. *Shin Oak Ridge.* Austin, Firm Foundation Publishing House, 1964.

Clancy, Foghorn. *My 50 Years in Rodeo.* San Antonio, Texas, Naylor Co., 1952.

Collings, Ellsworth and Alma Miller England. *The 101 Ranch.* Norman, University of Oklahoma Press, 1938.

Conrad, Barnaby. *How to Fight a Bull.* Garden City, New York, Doubleday and Co., 1968.

Day, Beth. *America's First Cowgirl, Lucille Mulhall.* New York, Jullian Messner Co., 1955.

Gibson, Fred. *Fabulous Empire.* Boston, Houghton Mifflin Co., 1946.

Harris, Foster. *The Look of the Old West.* New York, Viking Press, 1955.

Hendrick, John. *If I Can Do It on Horseback.* Austin, University of Texas Press, 1964.

Miller, H. E. L. *Minoan Crete.* New York, J. B. Putnam Sons., 1967.

North, Escott. *The Saga of the Cowboy.* New York, Jarrolds, 1942.

O'Brien, Esse Forrester. *That First Bulldogger.* San Antonio, Texas, Naylor and Co., 1961.

Osborn, Campbell. *Oklahoma Comes of Age.* Oklahoma City, Campbell Co., 1965.

Robertson, M. S. *Rodeo Standard Guide to the Cowboy Sport.* Berkeley, California, Nowell-North, 1961.

Rodeo Guide. Largo, Florida, Snibbe Sports Publication, Inc., 1968.

Rodeo Reference Book. Denver, Colorado, Rodeo Information Foundation, 1969 and 1970.

Russell, Don. *The Wild West.* Fort Worth, Texas, Amon Carter, Museum of Western Art, 1970.

Russell, Donald B. *The Lives and Legends of Buffalo Bill.* Norman, University of Oklahoma Press, 1960.

Shirley, Glenn. *Buckskin and Spurs.* New York, Hastings House, 1958.

Terry, Cleo Tom and Osie Wilson. *The Rawhide Tree.* Clarendon, Texas, Clarendon Press, 1957.

Towne, Charles W. and Edward Wentworth. *Cattle and Men.* Norman, University of Oklahoma Press, 1955.

Ward, Faye. *The Cowboy at Work.* New York, Hastings House, 1958.

Whitlock, V. H. *Cowboy Life on the Llano Estacado.* Norman, University of Oklahoma Press, 1970.

Woods, Pendleton. *Rodeo Champions Head for Oklahoma City.* Oklahoma City Chamber of Commerce, 1971.

Zemmerman, Dr. Charles LeRoy. *White Eagle Chief of the Poncas.* Harrisburg, Pennsylvania, Telegraph Press, 1941.

Articles

Armstrong, Jerry. "How the Calgary Stampede Began," *Old West,* Vol. VI, No. 3 (Spring, 1970).

Brown, Bob. "The West As It Was," *Western,* Vol. I, No. 4 (September-October, 1969).

———. "Cow Country Companeros," *Oklahoma Today,* Vol. XX, No. 3 (Summer, 1970).

Coffey, Ivy. "Former Hands at 101 Ranch Reminisce at Reunion," *Daily Oklahoman,* August 29, 1969.

Gill, Gale. "Texas Trail Ride, Negro Cowboys," *Ebony,* May 1963, 115-120.

Henderson, Sam. "Lorena Tricky Rodeo's Bonanza," *The West,* Vol. VII, No. 4 (September, 1967).

Hinkle, Milt. "A Texan Hits the Pampas," *Old West,* Vol. II, No. 1 (Fall, 1965).

———. "Bulldoggers," *True West,* Vol. XV, No. 2 (November-December 1967).

———. "Early Day Rodeo Circuits," *Old West,* Vol. VI, No. 2 (Winter, 1969).

———. "Spradley of the 101," *True West,* Vol. XII, No. 1 (September-October, 1964).

———. "The Dusky Demon," *True West,* Vol. VIII, No. 6 (July-August, 1961).

———. "The Dusky Demon; The Human Bulldog," *Rodeo News* (September, 1965).

Jackson, Donald. "Memories of Big Country," *Life,* Vol. LXVIII, No. 12 (April 3, 1970).

Katigan, Madelon B. "The Fabulous 101," *True West,* Vol. VIII, No. 1 (September-October, 1960).

Kirk, Bill. "Cowboy Stigall Can Look Back on Beginnings of Rodeos in Area," *Ponca City News,* September 16, 1964.

Lutz, Aleta. "The 101 Ranch and the Buffalo Bulldogger," *Oklahoma Today* (Summer, 1962), pp. 6-7.

McGaw, Bill. "Rangler Tells How Cowboy Bill Pickett Wrestled a Fighting Bull," *Southwesterner,* July 19, 1962.

———. "Southwest Rodeos Held Early in 1847," *Southwesterner* (February, 1967).

Mundis, Jerrold J. "He Took the Bull by the Horns," *American Heritage,* Vol. XIX, No. 1 (December, 1967).

Patch, Charlie C. "Negro Cowboy," *Real West,* Vol. XI, No. 64 (October 18, 1915).

Porter, Willard H. "Pickett Really Started Something," *The Cattleman* (September, 1953).

Preece, Harold. "American Negro Cowboys," *Real West,* Vol. IX, No. 45 (January, 1966).

Reedy, Ben I. "Wrestling Steers Behind the Barrier," *Rodeo News* (June, 1966).

Reynolds, Chang. "101 Ranch Wild West Show," *Bandwagon*, Vol. XIII, No. 1 (January-February 1969).

Risien, E. C. "To the Editor," *Life*, Vol. LXVIII, No. 15.

Rodeo Historical Society, *News Bulletin*, Vol. 1, No. 15 (September, 1968).

Secrest, William B. "Black Man's West," *True Frontier*, Vol. 1, No. 12 (November, 1969).

Shirley, Glenn D. "Bill Pickett The Man Who Developed Bulldogging," *Golden West*, Vol. 20, No. 1 (November, 1964).

———. "The First Bulldogger," *Western*, Vol. 1, No. 5 (November-December, 1969).

———. "The Man Who Invented Bulldogging," *Grit*, June 21, 1959.

Stewart, Roy P. "The Role of Negro in American West Being Told," *Daily Oklahoman*, July 21, 1967.

Thetford, Francis. "O. U. Librarian Holds Hammer Lock on Origin in Ancient Art of Bulldogging," *Daily Oklahoman*, February 15, 1968.

The Wild Bunch, Vol. 2, No. 4 (September, 1916).

Willson, Roscoe. "The First Bulldogger." *Arizona Days*, January 28, 1968.

Interviews with the Author

Ballew, James (Jim) O., January 3, 1970.

Beeson, Fred, April 24, 1970.

Fairley, Rev. S. Sylvester, April 10, 1970.

Feary, Mrs. Don, July 2, 1968 and August 1, 1968.

Gordon, Oral, June 26, 1969.

Hendrick, G. H., June 15, 1965 and December 25, 1965.

Laird, Jackie, October 30, 1969.

Lewis, Walton, November 1, 1969 and April 25, 1970.

Muchmore, Garieth, April 16, 1969.

Pickett, Alberta, February 22, 1970.

Randolph, Floyd, October 25, 1969.

Schultz, Mrs. Sonny, April 16, 1969.

Schultz, Walter, November 1, 1969.
Woods, R. S., February 8, 1969.

Letters

Ahlgreen, A. M. (City Clerk, Taylor, Texas), to Author, September 12, 1966.

Baker, Mrs. Mary (Prescott Chamber of Commerce, Prescott, Arizona), to Author, May 27, 1969.

Baskin, Jack, to Author, October 3, 1969.

Bender, Billy Sr., to Author, January 23, 1969; February 2, 1969.

Bender, Billy Sr., to Rodeo Historical Society, January 2, 1969; January 4, 1969; January 14, 1969; April 14, 1969; June 17, 1969.

Binotti, Col. Albert E. (Texas State Adjutant General's Department), to Author, March 24, 1969.

Brophy, Mrs. Marion (New York State Historical Association), to Author, August 4, 1969.

Bryson, Dr. J. Gordon, to Author, September 1, 1966; September 9, 1966; September 12, 1966; September 14, 1966.

Cameron, Goldie, to Author, May 5, 1968.

Carroll, W. D. (State Registrar, Texas State Department of Health), to Author, February 25, 1970.

Carson, Donald R., to Author, May 27, 1969.

Chrisman, Mrs. Mildred, to Author, January 28, 1969.

Cooley, Marguerite B. (Director, Library and Archives—State of Arizona), to Author, July 11, 1968.

Corkran, Charles W. (Texas State Archives), to Author, September 11, 1967.

Cotton, Robert, to Author, July 16, 1968.

Day, James M. (Director of State Archives, Texas State Library), to Author, August 19, 1966.

Deak, Dr. Edmond, to Author, June 22, 1962.

Dellinger, J. W., to Author, January 24, 1966; November 1, 1966; August 19, 1968.

Dill, C. A., to Author, July 3, 1968; July 22, 1968.

Ellis, Mary Jane (San Antonio Public Library, San Antonio, Texas), to Author, May 19, 1966.

Fireman, Bert M. (Curator, Arizona Collection, Arizona State University), to Author, July 1, 1968.

Fleischer, Mary Beth (Baker, Texas History Library), to Author, September 11, 1967.

Fletcher, Mrs. Cheryl, to Author, May 16, 1968.

Fletcher, Frances, to Author, October 9, 1968; January 30, 1969; July 9, 1969.

Friend, Florence (Librarian, Baker, Texas History Library), to Author, August 18, 1966.

Garrett, Sam, to Author, April 4, 1966; July 15, 1968; February 24, 1970.

Haines, LaRue, to Author, March 25, 1970.

Haley, Jack D. (University of Oklahoma Western History Collection), to Author, April 24, 1969.

Hall, John M., to Author, April 1, 1969.

Halverson, Katherine (Chief, Research, Wyoming State Archives), to Author, June 2, 1969.

Hammons, Dorothy (Office Manager, Pendleton Round-up Association), to Author, May 14, 1969.

Henderson, Sam, to Glen W. Farish, 1968.

Highfell, Kathleen, to Author, June 13, 1969.

Hinkle, Milt, to Author, December 14, 1965; September 23, 1967; March 26, 1968; April 30, 1969.

Hislin, James J. (The New York Historical Society), to Author, August 8, 1969.

Holmes, Nannie Pickett, to Author, August 12, 1966; August 23, 1966; June 15, 1968.

Kenny, John M. (Texas Archives), to Author, May 20, 1969.

Kiamer, Garrett (Director, Benjamin Franklin Library, Mexico, D.F.), to Author, April 14, 1969.

King, Alberta Pickett, to Author, February 2, 1970; March 3, 1970.

Koller, Joe (Secretary, Black Hills Round-Up), to Author, May 17, 1969.

Lewis, Walton, to Author, November 30, 1969.

Miller, Jack A. (Administrative Director, Cheyenne Frontier Days), to Author, April 30, 1969; May 21, 1969.

Muchmore, Gareth, to Author, May 24, 1966.

Mundy, Irby D., to Author, October 2, 1968.

McCracken, Jack, to Author, February 3, 1969.

McElry, John Sr., to Author, May 20, 1969.

McGehee, Elva, to Author, May 25, 1969.

Parkinson, Robert L. (Circus World Museum), to Author, October 25, 1967; January 11, 1968; May 29, 1968; April 20, 1969; September 3, 1969; March 18, 1970.

Pfening, Fred D. Jr. (Publisher, *Bandwagon*), to Author, May 24, 1969; March 25, 1970.

Ponder, Richard L., to Author, May 23, 1968.

Reynolds, Florence, to Author, September 29, 1969.

Ross, Ruby Pickett, to Author, May 12, 1968; May 20, 1968.

Sark, Elmer J., to Author, June 21, 1968; October 7, 1968.

Saunders, T. B., to Author, June 23, 1969.

Smith, Chuck (Publisher, *Rodeo News*), to Author, November 28, 1966.

Smith, Don L., to Author, June 5, 1968.

Smith, The Reverend W. Angie (Bishop of Oklahoma Conference, Methodist Church), to Author, June 20, 1968.

Timmons, Mrs. Alice M. (Phillips Collection, University of Oklahoma Library), to Author, August 7, 1968; September 15, 1968.

Trego, Dr. Gustavo A. Perez (Director, Hemertica National, Mexico, D.F.), to Author, June 13, 1969; January 1, 1970; January 22, 1970.

Wagner, Pat, to Author, June 6, 1969.

Ward, Faye E., to Author, December 3, 1966.

Whitworth, Robert L. (Ponca City Chamber of Commerce, Ponca City, Oklahoma), to Author, May 24, 1966.

Wilkes, T., to Author, June 22, 1969.

Newspapers

Arizona Republican, Phoenix, Arizona, May 25, 1969.

Birmingham News, Birmingham, Alabama, May 13, 1969.

Boston Sunday Advertiser, Boston, Massachusetts, June 8, 1969.

Chicago Daily News, Chicago, Illinois, August 19, 1916.

Chicago Herald, Chicago, Illinois, August 18-20, 1916.

Daily Oklahoman, Oklahoma City, Oklahoma, July 21 and 27, November 23, 1967; February 15, 1968; August 29, 1969.

Denver Post, Denver, Colorado, August 30-31, 1908.

El Diavio, Mexico City, D.F., December 10, 22, and 24, 1908.

El Impractical, Mexico City, D.F., December 23 and 24, 1908.

Guthrie Daily Leader, Guthrie, Oklahoma, October 17, 1968.

Kansas City Journal, Kansas City, Missouri, August 29, September 2-4, 1916.

Kansas City Post, Kansas City, Missouri, August 31, September 1, 3 and 4, 1916.

Kansas City Star, Kansas City, Missouri, August 27 and 31, 1916.

Kansas City Times, Kansas City, Missouri, September 1 and 2, 1916.

Mexican Herald, Mexico City, D.F., December 22-24, 1908.

Ponca City News, Ponca City, Oklahoma, June 3, 1926; February 27, 1928; April 2 and 4, October 4, 1932; September 14, 1949; September 16, 1965; September 15, 1968.

Sacramento Bee, Sacramento, California, May 18, 1969.

Taylor Daily Press, Taylor, Texas, November 23, 1956.

Times, London, England, May 25, 1914.

Wyoming Tribune, Cheyenne, Wyoming, August 29-September 1, 1904.

Yale News, Yale, Oklahoma, August 21, 1969.

Miscellaneous

Bulletin—Pickett Brothers, Broncho Busters and Rough Riders Association, Taylor, Texas.

Certificate of Death, Oklahoma State Board of Health. Bill Pickett.

Georgetown Chamber of Commerce, Georgetown, Texas, History of Williamson County.

Griffith, J. H. "Sketches of Early Days in Taylor." January 12, 1923.

Honorees, National Rodeo Hall of Fame, January 24, 1964, 1972.

Information received from Zack Miller Jr. and Gareth Muchmore, April, 1923.

Marriage License, Williamson County, Texas, December 1, 1890, William Pickett and Maggie Williams

Memorandum from Court Clerk, Kay County, Oklahoma, July 11, 1969.

National Cowboy Hall of Fame and Western Heritage Center Brochure, June 26, 1965.

Official Program of Miller Brothers, Arlington 101 Ranch Wild West Show of 1910.

Pickett's Birth and Death from Ruby Pickett Ross's personal records.

Questionnaire to Sam Garrett, October 18, 1968.

Records of County Clerk, Williamson County, Texas, October 18, 1968.

Subpoena — State of Oklahoma vs. Bill Pickett, County of Kay, Case No. 5768, November 17, 1926.

INDEX

197